December 1995

Merry Christmas Buddy.

Lots

Dad

The FRIENDSHIP BOOK

of Francis Gay

D. C. THOMSON & CO., LTD.
London   Glasgow   Manchester   Dundee

A Thought
For Each Day
in 1996

*Of all the things which wisdom
provides to make life entirely
happy, much the greatest is the
possession of friendship.*

Epicurus.

ON THE
RIGHT ROAD

JANUARY

<u>MONDAY—JANUARY 1.</u>

SITTING contentedly in my armchair after an excellent New Year lunch cooked by the Lady of the House, I reflected with gratitude on my own good fortune. That's why I'm passing on a selection of the old adages I've collected on the theme of kitchens and cooking, as a tribute to all who have lovingly prepared food for us this Festive Season — and indeed throughout the year:

A housewife sweet, a kitchen neat,
There you can find good things to eat.

A good dinner is better than a fine coat.

One cake eaten in peace is worth two in trouble.

Hospitality polishes the pots.

A good dinner sharpens the wit and softens the
*   heart.*

For the food that we eat and those who prepare it,
For health to enjoy it and for friends to share it,
We thank Thee O Lord.

<u>TUESDAY—JANUARY 2.</u>

THE Sunday School teacher was rounding off her weekly lesson. "So that's the story of Jonah and the whale. What does it teach us?" she asked.

The prompt reply came at once: "You can't keep a good man down!"

Unusual, but perhaps not too inaccurate!

THE FRIENDSHIP BOOK

TO A NEW YEAR

MY God, I come to you in this new year,
Unknowing in the dark, the way unclear,
And yet in faith I take my way with you,
  In certain trust that you will see me through.
I bring to you the labour of my hands,
  A supple will to bend to your commands,
My span of years as you see fit to give,
  My love in good or ill while I shall live.
I bring to you the soul you gave to me,
  My hopes for all the days that are to be,
My faithful worship in your holy place,
  One thing I ask, that you will give me grace.

Anon.

THE Lady of the House always has a five-year diary, and it is written up every day without fail. It means something very special to her — there are notes about friends, the weather, animals, the garden, our holidays, and there are even some jokes. All the things in life that most of us take for granted are recorded and cherished.

Every New Year she looks through it, often with a chuckle, and reads passages to me with great delight and interest. We both find that these diaries are a never-ending source of memories.

What better way can there be to start New Year than to recall fond memories of the past, and reflect on our hopes for the future?

"Thankful for all that has been
And trustful for all that's to come."

I WAS given this plan for a New Year vegetable garden, one you'll surely like to cultivate:

"First plant five rows of peas: Preparedness, promptness, perseverance, politeness and prayer.

"Next to them plant three rows of squash: Squash gossip, squash criticism, squash indifference.

"Then put in five rows of lettuce: Let us be faithful; let us be unselfish; let us be loyal; let us love one another; let us be truthful.

"No garden is complete without turnips and the New Year version should have: Turn up for church; turn up with a smile; turn up with a new idea; turn up with real determination."

FLORENCE NIGHTINGALE was a great person, but I sometimes think that those unsung, anonymous volunteers were even greater. Florence was a great organiser, a marvellous mediator between numerous government departments of the day, but without her devoted band of helpers she could not have accomplished the work for which she alone has become a household name.

Isn't it often the same in life? The "little person" can so easily be overlooked. We should try to give credit to these unnoticed heroes and heroines!

BE still, and know that I am God: I will be exalted among the heathen, I will be exalted in the earth. The Lord of hosts is with us; the God of Jacob is our refuge. Selah.

Psalms 46:10-11

WHITE AND BRIGHT

THE FRIENDSHIP BOOK

THE Lady of the House and I called to see our friend Mary on a gloomy January day. There had been a spell of freezing fog and ice, and we were concerned to check that she had everything necessary for her comfort.

Mary was her usual cheerful and serene self, all the same. Her fire was glowing, the radio was playing softly in the background and it wasn't long before we were all enjoying tea and hot buttered toast in her cosy sitting-room.

"Lots of people would be feeling sorry for themselves in this weather," remarked the Lady of the House. "What is your secret, Mary?"

"Well," replied our old friend, "as long as I am preoccupied with worrying about what *might* happen, I can't enjoy what *is* happening."

There's something about an afternoon with Mary that makes her visitors feel *they* are the ones who have benefited from the visit!

HERE is a clipping sent by a friend from her church magazine:

If you should find the Perfect Church
Without one fault or smear,
For goodness sake, don't join that church,
You'd spoil the atmosphere.
But since no perfect church exists
Where people never sin,
Let's cease in looking for that church,
And love the one we're in!

If we tried to apply that philosophy within our family, our friendships or our place of work, what a difference it could make!

THE FRIENDSHIP BOOK

WEDNESDAY—JANUARY 10.

"**D**OESN'T the room look bare!" exclaimed the Lady of the House.

Of course, she was right. Twelfth Night had come and gone and all the Christmas decorations were packed away in their boxes.

However, we soon gave ourselves a shake. The year was still young, and no one could know what the coming months would bring. It was a fresh start, a voyage on an uncharted sea.

Suddenly, the depression slipped away and a new sense of excitement took its place. I remembered some lines I found a few weeks before:

When Christmas is over, the real work begins —
To help the lost and the lonely,
To seek for peace,
To plant a seed of happiness wherever we can.

Perhaps we can play a small part in this very valuable work, not just after Christmas, but all through the year.

THURSDAY—JANUARY 11.

RUDYARD KIPLING, the famous poet, went to live in the USA and set up house on the side of a valley.

One day he went out walking, and after a long tramp found himself at a lonely and isolated farmhouse on the opposite side. Here he got into conversation with a woman who asked, "Are you the new lights across the valley? You won't know what a comfort they've been to me this Winter when I felt alone and cut off. You won't ever put them out, will you?"

We never know how influential our actions may be — perhaps affecting a person we don't even know.

LAKE LAND

SOMETIMES life thrusts unwelcome changes on us and it is natural to feel dispirited or sad. At such times it is worth remembering an old saying:

"When one door of happiness closes another opens, but often we look so long at the closed door that we do not see the other one."

SATURDAY—JANUARY 13.

IN spite of profound deafness, Kerena Marchant has achieved a successful career within the BBC Religious Broadcasts Department, and she has been involved in many of the "Songs Of Praise" programmes.

Being deaf has perhaps made her more sensitive to the problems of others than is usual in a young person. In the story of her life she wrote: "I can be feeling really depressed about something and meet a cheerful person, who has nothing to be cheerful about, and their happiness washes on to me and makes me realise that my problems are very minor."

It's a lovely gift to be able to share with others and reminds me of a jotting from my notebook:

I'm telling you it's odd but true,
the richest folk are not
The ones who always like to boast
about the wealth they've got.
The rich are kindly folk who smile,
and warm our hearts a little while.

SUNDAY—JANUARY 14.

HE that hath ears to hear, let him hear.
Matthew 11:15

MONDAY—JANUARY 15.

WHEN I succumbed to a dose of flu, I was only too willing to retire to bed and seek comfort in the healing properties of sleep.

Reflecting on it later, I found that Cervantes had written this about sleep:

"Sweet dreams. God bless whoever invented sleep, the mantle that embraces the thoughts of all men, food that satisfies all hunger, the weight that balances the scales and makes the shepherd the same as the king, the fool the same as the wise man."

However, it was Victor Hugo I feel who put the whole subject in perspective. He wrote: "Have courage for the great sorrows of life and patience for the small ones. When you have laboriously accomplished your daily tasks, go to sleep. God is awake."

TUESDAY—JANUARY 16.

HOW very true are these thoughts on happiness below.

William Riley, the Yorkshire novelist, wrote in one of his stories: "Happiness is a plant that will grow in any soil that is watered by love and service, but withers in the hot sun of selfishness."

When Ralph Waldo Emerson, the great American essayist, wrote about happiness he said: "For every minute you are angry you lose sixty seconds of happiness."

So, as William Riley tells us, happiness grows with unselfishness, and Emerson knew that anger can lose us nearly a lifetime of happiness if stored away in our hearts. Life will be a lot happier, for us and the people we encounter in our journey through this world, if we remember these wise words.

WEDNESDAY—JANUARY 17.

HERE is another selection of twenty-second sermons — those sayings with few words but a big message:

Words should be weighted not counted.

A journey of a thousand miles must begin with a single step.

Never measure the height of a mountain until you have reached the top. Then you will see how low it was.   (Dag Hammerskjold)

Hope is like the sun which as we journey towards it, casts the shadow of our burden behind us.

It takes more grace than man can tell
To play the second fiddle well.

THURSDAY—JANUARY 18.

IN Fairford Church, off the main Gloucester to Wantage road, are 28 beautifully-painted glass windows, all dating from the 15th century. They are admired by visitors from near and far.

In Fairford churchyard there is a stone effigy in memory of someone who actually lived in that village church for 15 years!

Tiddles was a tabby cat who faithfully attended the services at Fairford church and caught lots of mice and other small prey. She was looked after and fed by the verger, and when she died in 1980, he commissioned a stone effigy for Fairford's attractive churchyard.

His comment speaks for itself: "She spent more time in the church than anyone else — and she deserved a burial plot of her own."

WHEN our friend, Muriel, failed her driving test for the fourth time she was devastated. She rang her mother saying she had failed yet again, but her mother's reply was, "Remember, dear. You've never failed until you've given up trying."

Muriel says that these words have helped her on innumerable occasions when, not having reached her desired goal after several tries, she has been tempted to give up.

What a great help a few casual words spoken with sincerity can do. Perhaps you can encourage someone today.

SATURDAY—JANUARY 20.

SOME years ago there was a popular record called "The Deck Of Cards". Do you remember the story behind it?

An American soldier is caught playing cards in church, hauled before his commanding officer, but manages to talk himself out of trouble by relating features of a pack of cards to aspects of Scripture. Very ingenious! I was reminded of all this when I read a quote from writer Josh Billings:

"As in a game of cards, so in the game of life we must play with what is dealt out to us; and the glory consists not so much in winning as in playing a poor hand well."

SUNDAY—JANUARY 21.

AND the Word was made flesh, and dwelt among us, (and we beheld his glory, the glory as of the only begotten of the Father,) full of grace and truth.

John 1:14

MIST OPPORTUNITIES

THE FRIENDSHIP BOOK

SAUNTERING through a local market with the Lady of the House, our attention was caught by a misspelt notice: LADES JAKET.

I was reminded of a sign in a shop window which read: FISHING TICKLE. Noticing the error, a customer asked, "Hasn't anyone told you about it before?"

"Yes," replied the owner, "many have dropped in to tell me, and they often buy something."

Not far from where we live is a butcher's shop which has fresh notices every week, offering a prize to the person who spots the deliberate mistake. Then one of our friends has a wonderful time every Friday spotting the mistakes in his local paper.

Life sometimes seems full of mistakes! Some are deliberate, some are not. I have heard it said that it is these human foibles which endear men to their ladies, and ladies to their menfolk.

The world would be a poorer place if we didn't make mistakes at which we can laugh — and learn!

Don't you agree?

DID you hear the story of the professor, who just managed to catch a train as it was leaving a suburban railway station?

He jumped in and sat down thankfully next to a young girl. When he had recovered his breath, he realised that he was sitting on her newspaper. Drawing it from beneath him, he apologised profusely. The girl thanked him, but kept looking at him somewhat anxiously.

At the next station, she prepared to get out, and then said, "Please, sir, may I have my fish, too?"

THE FRIENDSHIP BOOK

I LOOK at a tree
Yet cannot see
What makes it grow.

I look at the sky
Much higher than high.
What makes it so?

I look at a babe
From nothing seen.
Who made it so?

I feel in my heart
That prayer was a part.
And now I know.

Harry Miller.

JANE has warm and welcoming brown eyes and she loves children, especially babies. It is a joy to watch the reaction she gets. They seem to respond to her expression, and in a very short time they are all smiles.

A baby's smile is one of the first means of communication with someone other than its mother, and Mother Teresa wrote a memorable piece on the value of being able to smile:

"Let there be kindness in your face, in your eyes and in the warmth of your greeting. For children, for the poor, for all who suffer and are alone, always have a happy smile. Give them not only your care but your heart."

In the often troubled world in which we live, let us remember Mother Teresa's words and make time to smile. It can have far-reaching effects.

FRIDAY—JANUARY 26.

WHEN a Cornish solicitor, Richard Tippett, heard that his favourite author Charles Dickens was to be guest of honour at a dinner in a local hotel, he was determined to see him. Alas, numbers were strictly limited and there was no chance of dining with his hero.

Then he had a brainwave. He persuaded the landlord to let him be one of the waiters!

All went well until, as the meal was drawing to a close, one of the guests tried to impress Dickens with a Latin quotation — and got it wrong.

"Excuse me, sir," said Tippett, "I think that the accent is on the 'e'."

Curious, Dickens questioned the "waiter" who confessed that he was not what he seemed. Dickens was highly amused and at once invited him to sit at the table and join him and the others for dessert.

It was to be the proudest moment of Richard Tippett's life — and all because he had taken a job serving people, when he was normally more used to being served.

SATURDAY—JANUARY 27.

WHAT a lot of time we can waste, worrying about things that may never happen! I've always been grateful to a wise old lady who gave me this advice:

"Never trouble trouble till trouble troubles you."

SUNDAY—JANUARY 28.

FOR wisdom is better than rubies; and all the things that may be desired are not to be compared to it.

Proverbs 8:11

THE FRIENDSHIP BOOK

A FRIEND found a part-time job as a canvasser, visiting homes for market research. At one house he was welcomed and he asked his first prepared question, "Who is the head of this household?"

"I'm the boss of this house," the husband replied, "and I have my wife's permission to say so."

My friend says it's a true story. It's a good one, anyway — and I have permission from the Lady of the House to pass it on!

"ANYONE can carry his burden, however hard, until nightfall. Anyone can do all his work, however hard, for one day. Anyone can live sweetly, patiently, lovingly, purely, till the sun goes down. And this is all that life really means."

Robert Louis Stevenson.

IT was only the end of January, and we still had a great deal of Winter to come.

However, dawn came a few minutes earlier that morning. There was some expectant chattering among the birds, and later there was a gardening programme on television showing the many varieties of blooms I could grow in my tubs and flower borders this year. I just ached to get out into the garden and make a start, and I didn't have to draw the curtains before afternoon tea that day.

Oh, yes, we are definitely approaching Springtime, so don't let the rest of Winter get you down. Brighter, warmer days are only round the corner, the start of a new chapter for us all.

FEBRUARY

THURSDAY—FEBRUARY 1.

I WONDER how *you* regard bringing up children? I read this apt comment in a church magazine recently:

"I see children as kites. You spend years trying to get them off the ground. You run with them until you are both breathless . . . they crash . . . they hit the rooftop . . . you patch, comfort and assure them that some day they will fly.

"Finally, they are airborne. They need more string and you keep letting it out, but with each twist of the ball of twine, there is a sadness that goes with joy. The kite becomes more distant and you know it won't be long before that beautiful creature will snap the lifeline that binds you together and will soar as it is meant to soar — free and alone. Only then do you know that you have done your job."

FRIDAY—FEBRUARY 2.

L EAFING through an old Methodist manual in a library one day, I found the suggestion that preachers should always keep to the point and concentrate on their theme.

John Wesley himself used this method, and his sermon on the use of money is still often quoted today. He said very concisely: "Gain all you can, Save all you can, Give all you can."

We should make a note from this old manual, especially if we have any advice to offer to others. Keep it short and to the point, and say it only once — then, like Wesley's message, it may be remembered for years.

THE FRIENDSHIP BOOK

I IMAGINE you know these lovely words:
"I expect to pass through this world, but once.
Any good deed, therefore, that I can do, or any
kindness that I can show to my fellow creatures, let me
do it *now*. Let me not defer or neglect it, for I shall not
pass this way again."

I am sure that Stephen Grellet's thoughts will
continue to be remembered — relevant sentiments for
yesterday, today and tomorrow.

B LESSED be the King that cometh in the name of
the Lord: peace in heaven, and glory in the
highest.

Luke 19:38

I T'S never too late to pay tribute to great courage.
In 1991 the people of Le Hohwald, in the Vosges
mountains of France, joined with friends to erect a
fountain in memory of a woman's bravery during the
Second World War.

Dr Adelaide Hautval, a native of the village, was
arrested in 1942 for going to the aid of a family being
ill-treated by Nazis in a railway station. The following
year she was sent to the concentration camp of
Auschwitz where she resolutely refused to take part in
"experiments" being made on the prisoners.

She survived the horrors of the camp and lived on
until 1988. Today the beautiful fountain recalls her
bravery. On it a few words are inscribed which,
translated, mean: "Think and act according to the
clear waters of your being".

DADDY'S GIRL

THE FRIENDSHIP BOOK

I LIKE the anonymous description of "My Way".

At home it is kindness . . .
In business it is honesty . . .
In society it is courtesy . . .
In work it is thoroughness . . .
In play it is fairness . . .
Toward the fortunate it is congratulations . . .
Toward the weak it is help . . .
Toward wickedness it is resistance . . .
Toward the penitent it is forgiveness . . .
Toward God it is reverence, love and obedience.

WHEN Minna Keal was a child she learned to play the piano and developed a great love of music. After leaving school she enrolled as a student at the Royal Academy of Music in London, but had to give it up when her father died. Instead, she married, and the whole of her working life was spent doing a routine factory job.

At the age of 66 when she was retired, she decided to use her pension as a "student grant" in order to study the composition of music, and so fulfil a dream that she had had for many years. Her third composition was a major symphony and it was played — and praised — at the Proms in 1989 when she was 80 years old.

As Minna said, "When you retire, you can do almost whatever you want to. I felt as if I was starting all over again, and now I live as if all my life is in front of me, not behind me."

It's a story to encourage anyone who feels they have a gift or talent hidden within them that hasn't had the opportunity to surface. It's never too late!

THE FRIENDSHIP BOOK

ISN'T it a nice feeling to handle something new? There is something special about it and how let down we would feel if we received a present that was second-hand. I remember Julie Andrews once sang "Second-Hand Rose", a song in which she bemoaned the fact that she never had things that were new.

As we get older, though, we begin to learn that something new is not always better. When I watch programmes about antiques on television, I'm often amazed at the valuations placed by experts on objects I would often have dismissed as "old junk".

I once read a piece by the writer Miles Kington which ended: "In some fields the old and used is valued more than the shiny and new." That applies not only to material things, but to old friendships which grow firmer and truer as the years go by.

SAILORS are well known for being romantic and here's a story to prove it.

Robin was on leave and spending the weekend at Jane's home. It was the annual church garden party and unknown to anybody else, Robin had arranged a little surprise with the man in charge of the lucky dip. When Jane's fishing line hooked on to a tiny package, she was amazed to find it contained a beautiful emerald ring.

"My word," she remarked, "that's good value for 20p!" She did not realise its significance until later.

The ring was proudly placed on her engagement finger. Robin and Jane have been happily married for many years now and the family joke, in which their sons share, is about the husband who was hooked for only 20p!

THE FRIENDSHIP BOOK

WHEN we visit Derbyshire, the Lady of the House and I often come across youngsters abseiling. It always looks so breathtaking. I can never see myself hanging over a cliff top, depending on a length of rope to get me to the ground, but it is a technique enjoyed by many climbers.

On one of my gentle climbs I was watching some of these folk, and suddenly thought of how we should put our trust in God, just as the abseilers were putting all their trust in their leaders, who will always stand firm and can be relied on to hold them safely.

Experiences in life have sometimes made me feel that I am falling over a cliff edge; but in the end He has always been there to help and to hold me.

WHEREFORE gird up the loins of your mind, be sober, and hope to the end for the grace that is to be brought unto you at the revelation of Jesus Christ.

Peter I 1:13

KAREN needed to phone the clinic to make an appointment for an X-ray for her mother. She went to the telephone, dialled the number quickly, and as soon as a female voice answered at the other end, said, "Good morning, I'm ringing about my mother . . ."

The voice at the other end interrupted, "Are you sure you want us — this is the knacker's yard!"

After much hysterical laughter at both ends of the telephone, they eventually hung up . . .

THE FRIENDSHIP BOOK

ARE we ever satisfied? If we live in one room, we long for a flat; if we live in a flat, we long for a house; if we live in a house, we long for a mansion!

Yet, no matter how dissatisfied we may be with our lot, I guarantee there are two things you can have which will be welcome and the same in a one-room flat as in a palace — a cup of tea, while seated in an easy chair — because this means comfort, relaxation, rest and pleasure.

Put the kettle on, and enjoy yourself.

I WONDER if you are like me and find it difficult to resist having a peep through somebody's sitting-room window when lamps are lit and curtains still undrawn? Somehow or other it gives a tantalising glimpse of another person's private world.

Perhaps that is why TV programmes showing us the secret corners of other people's gardens are so popular. Once, through the eye of the camera, I saw several gardens where each owner had a passion for a particular variety of flower. The flowering passion of Freddy and Shasi Lambert was the lily, and their Sussex garden contained a profusion of these exotic blooms in every imaginable colour.

When Freddy was asked what had been in his mind when he had planned the garden 16 years ago, he said, "It was to bring a smile to my wife's face and to keep it there. Gardens are full of love and I want to keep a romantic atmosphere. I am 70 now and I'm still a romantic at heart."

It's a lovely thought to keep with us on St Valentine's Day, so I raise my hat to all those who — whatever age they may be — are romantics at heart.

C

THE FRIENDSHIP BOOK

I CAN'T vouch for the truth of this story, but it did appear in a church magazine, I can assure you.

A baby had been brought to church to be christened and as is usual, the parents had been asked to "Name this child". The vicar wasn't sure what the father had said, so he asked him to repeat it. Getting the same answer as before, the child was duly christened "Spin Donna".

It wasn't until after the service that the parents told him that what had actually been said was, "It's pinned on her."

TELL THEM NOW

GIVE praise to people young and old,
Encourage them while they're near;
For when they've gone to their reward,
Your loudest praise they will not hear.

D.M. Thorneloe.

I LIKE the story of Ambrose Paré, the brilliant 16th-century French surgeon who served in the armies of three kings — Henry II, Charles IX, and Henry III. He operated on hundreds of soldiers with gunshot wounds at a time when such injuries frequently became gangrenous.

He was a deeply compassionate and humble man, and history records that when complimented on the excellence of his work and the number of soldiers who recovered, his reply was: "I only dressed their wounds. It was God who healed them."

THE FRIENDSHIP BOOK

AND Jesus said unto them, I am the bread of life: he that cometh to me shall never hunger: and he that believeth on me shall never thirst.

John 6:35

"I'VE remembered a verse you'll like," said old Mary when the Lady of the House and I went into her cosy room during a recent visit. We did indeed like it, and here it is:

Count your garden by the flowers,
Never by the leaves that fall;
Count your days by golden hours,
Don't remember clouds at all.
Count your nights by stars, not shadows,
Count your life with smiles, not tears,
And with joy through all your journeys
Count your age by friends, not years.

THIS message was part of the farewell letter from a minister leaving his charge:

"Love one another — support and encourage one another; don't contaminate the atmosphere with unkind words and acts; look out for ways to help one another, and get on and do it; take time to enjoy one another's company; recognise and encourage one another's differing gifts."

What good advice it is, and something that could be profitable to all of us, wherever we may find ourselves today. To put it in a nutshell, give a little love and the world can be a better place.

THE FRIENDSHIP BOOK

YOU are reading this, so you are alive! Truly, what a wonderful gift life is. We are meant to enjoy it, so be certain that you make the most of this day — now. Fill every moment with good and happy thoughts and deeds, then in the future this lovely quotation will prove as true for you as it did for the original writer:

"God gave us memories so that we might have roses in December."

A MINISTER was staying a night in the home of a young couple. In the morning his hostess was singing in the kitchen, "Nearer, my God, to Thee".

At breakfast he said how he enjoyed hearing hymns sung around the house, but had never heard that lovely one sung so fast before.

His hostess replied, "Oh, that's because I don't pay attention to the words. It's a song my mother used to sing, and I've found that it's a good one to boil the eggs by. You repeat the first verse five times rapidly for soft boiled, and eight times for hard!"

THE Irish writer and sportsman, Lord Dunsany, once shot four woodcock and posted them to a friend as a culinary treat. The friend received the label that had been tied to the parcel, but nothing else.

On hearing of this, Dunsany went out and bagged four more woodcock. He parcelled them and sent them to his friend, this time attaching a label which read, "FOUR DEAD RATS". They were delivered in double-quick time!

MOUNTAIN MAJESTY

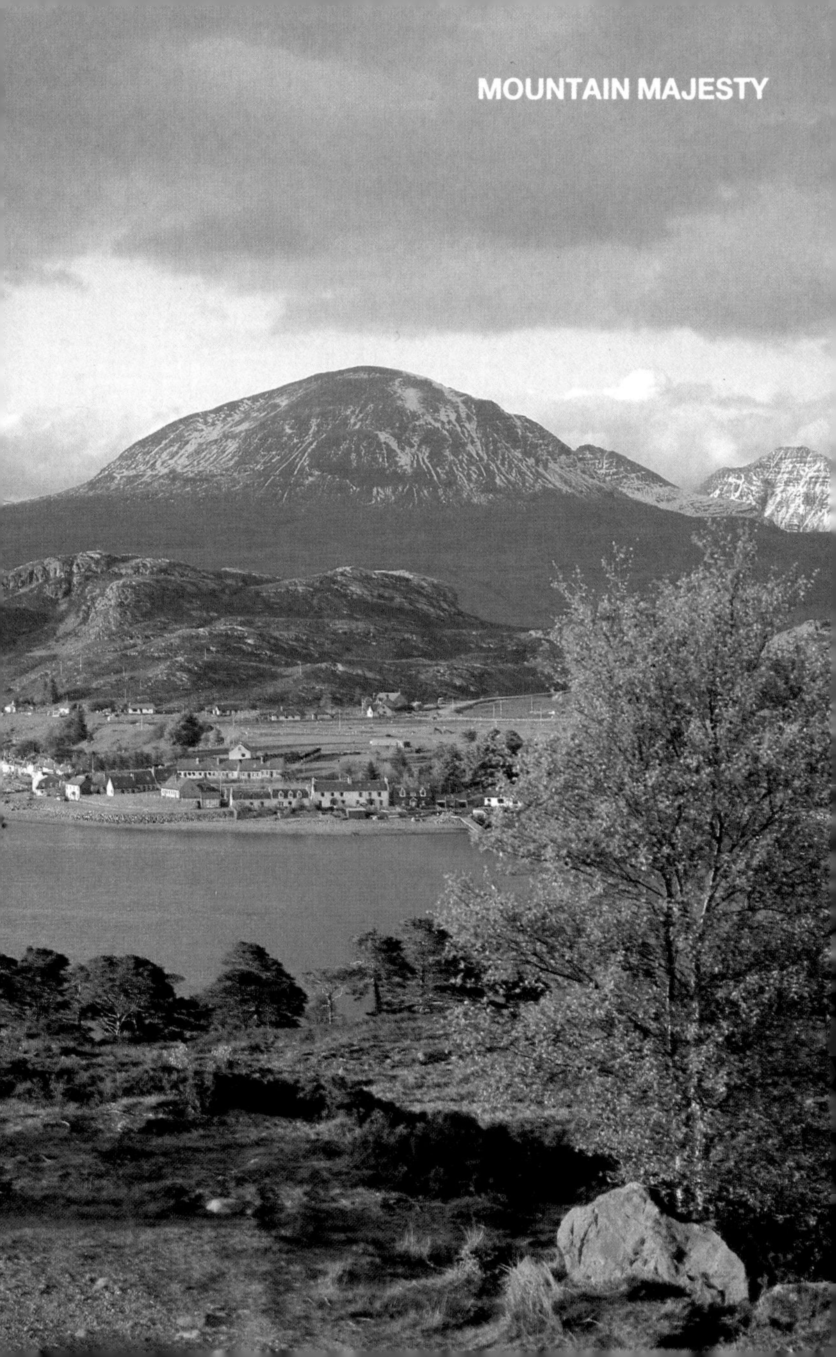

THE FRIENDSHIP BOOK

SATURDAY—FEBRUARY 24.

I LIKE the "Ten Rules For Success" which a friend in the USA sent to me:

Find your own particular talent.
Be big.
Be honest.
Live with enthusiasm.
Don't let your possessions possess you.
Don't worry about your problems.
Look up to people when you can — look down on no one.
Don't cling to the past.
Assume your full share of responsibility in the world.
Pray consistently and confidently.

SUNDAY—FEBRUARY 25.

AND God called the dry land Earth; and the gathering together of the waters called he Seas: and God saw that it was good.

Genesis 1:10

MONDAY—FEBRUARY 26.

AN editor, I know, receives many articles, but has to return most of them.

One disappointed and bitter person wrote back: "Sir, you sent back a story of mine. I know that you did not even read it because, as a test, I pasted together pages 19 and 20. The manuscript came back with those pages still stuck together, so I know that you are a fraud."

The reply came back: "Dear Madam, at breakfast when I open an egg, I don't have to eat it all to determine if it's bad."

THE FRIENDSHIP BOOK

LISTENING to "Thought For The Day" on the radio one morning, I heard the speaker say that we all have a divine spark, which in some cases needs regenerating. This reminded me of our gas cooker which had lost its spark.

The automatic ignition had broken, so I bought a box of matches, generating a spark manually. Since that broadcast, whenever I strike a match, I say to myself, "Have you generated *your* divine spark today? Are you ignited into doing something worthwhile?"

Although, like our cooker, parts of me have seen better days, I hope I can still perform some useful service to others, and I try to make sure I always have a metaphorical box of matches handy.

THE minister had said, "We will end our service with a hymn."

Afterwards as he shook hands at the church porch, a young man corrected him. "That was the end of the *worship*," he said quietly, "now starts the *service*."

SOME time ago I came across these lines about the weather, which I find most uplifting:

Whether the weather be fine,
  Or whether the weather be not,
Whether the weather be cold,
  Or whether the weather be hot,
We'll weather the weather,
  Whatever the weather,
Whether we like it or not.

MARCH

FRIDAY—MARCH 1.

AT the turn of the century when Edith Holden was compiling her "Country Diary", she was confident of finding woodlands carpeted with primroses each Spring. Sadly, during and after those years the flowers were indiscriminately picked and nowadays they are a protected species, to prevent them dying out altogether.

Long ago the primrose was known for its healing powers. It was used in salads as a cure for arthritis and the ointment made from its leaves was considered beneficial for burns and ulcers.

German people had a tradition that carrying a primrose provided an "open sesame" to hidden treasures and that is why they called it the "key flower". In the past, primroses were always thought of as magical. Known by country folk as fairy cups, it was believed that fairies lived within them and used them as a shelter when it rained.

People no longer leave a primrose on the doorstep on May Day Eve to keep away witches. Nowadays, after the bleakness of Winter, the real magic of the primrose is the welcome sight it brings in our first view of Spring.

SATURDAY—MARCH 2.

THE Lady of the House found this thought in a book she was reading.

"Words slip easily from the tongue. Think well before you let them go."

Surely a thought for *every* day.

THE FRIENDSHIP BOOK

HONOUR thy father and thy mother: and, Thou shalt love thy neighbour as thyself.

Matthew 19:19

TUESDAY—MARCH 4.

ANNIE PATTERSON was telling me about a gift she'd received from her young grandson. He'd been given his own small patch of garden to cultivate, and Annie had spent much time admiring it.

"I wish my garden looked as good as yours, David," she told him, "but I just don't have time."

She had thought no more about her remark until a week later when David arrived on her doorstep bearing three small flower-pots — each one containing a different variety of thyme!

"I didn't have the heart to explain the mistake," laughed Annie, "and in a way, it did work. Afterwards, I felt honour-bound to make my garden look better, just to show David that his gift wasn't wasted. Now I can truthfully say that a little thyme was indeed all I needed."

TUESDAY—MARCH 5.

OFTEN we make up our mind to do something — and then do nothing. We can't bring ourselves to make a start. It's too daunting. At such times I remember the words of the Latin poet, Horace:

"He has half the deed done who has made a beginning."

If that doesn't do the trick I think of this Dutch proverb:

"He who is outside his door has already a hard part of his journey behind him."

Then I begin!

THE FRIENDSHIP BOOK

"SPRING cleaning time!" announced the Lady of the House one day. I suppressed a groan and managed a weak smile instead.

I really love Spring, finding it the most cheerful and hopeful time of the year. However, Spring cleaning is quite another matter. The Lady of the House is not content merely to wash paintwork and change bedspreads. She likes to have a completely ruthless tidy-out, from the attic to the basement.

Often she will appear at my elbow with assorted articles and ask, "Do we really need these things?"

If I reply, "They could be useful," there is a stony silence of disbelief, then the objects in question are deposited by my chair for further inspection.

Once I found a church magazine from the previous Spring and stopped to read the message for Lent. Our minister considered that today's view of the weeks before Easter differed from the old belief in fasting and giving up those things that we most enjoy. His interpretation was more modern, suggesting that we take a closer look at ourselves. In fact, he described Lent as a "Spring cleaning of the soul."

I agreed and on reflection, had to admit that the Lady of the House had the right idea. We all accumulate so much trivia in our homes — and in our minds — that a really thorough Spring clean is just the thing that we all need!

I WONDER if we'd recover from business recessions a little more quickly by heeding this sign I spotted recently:

If you are like a wheelbarrow, going no farther than you are pushed, then do not apply to work here.

THE FRIENDSHIP BOOK

THE minster of our church has always emphasised the value of a positive discipline during Lent.

He feels that it shouldn't be regarded as a negative business of doing without sweets, or chocolates — or anything else. Rather it should include positive approaches such as reading a religious book — or visiting some lonely person, or hosting or sharing in a discussion group with members of a church fellowship.

Add positive comments to what you say about people; instead of suggesting that someone is very nice, *but* . . . why not say that someone is very nice *and* . . .?

There's a positive difference to be made by us all, if only we try.

TWO quotations about books caught my eye recently. The first was a Chinese proverb:

"A book is like a garden carried in the pocket."

The other was written by Kathleen Norris:

"Just the knowledge that a good book is awaiting one at the end of a long day makes that day happier."

I like to think that, for many of you, "The Friendship Book" is a garden you look forward to visiting every day.

GREAT is the Lord, and greatly to be praised in the city of our God, in the mountain of his holiness. Beautiful for situation, the joy of the whole earth, is mount Zion, on the sides of the north, the city of the great King.

Psalms 48:1-2

THE FRIENDSHIP BOOK

AT school one wet playtime five-year-old Tim fell in the playground. He went back into school weeping, wet through and covered in mud. His teacher came to the rescue. "Tim, however did you manage to make such a mess of yourself?"

"It was easy, miss," came the reply!

I hope that it won't happen to Tim, but as we grow older, maybe you have noticed that because of either our own bad luck or making what turns out to be a wrong decision, we sometimes fall into the mud and life seems to go awry. It can happen so easily.

It is at times like this we should always remember that we have an equally concerned and friendly Teacher like Tim's to pick us up, dust us down and set us on the right road again.

DO you like reading love stories? Whenever I see an avenue of white almond or cherry trees in the Springtime, I am reminded of a lovely legend from Portugal.

A Portuguese prince fell in love with a beautiful Scandinavian princess and brought her across the sea to the Algarve to be his wife. The princess dearly loved her husband and her new country, but Portugal has much less snow and she missed the snow-covered mountains of her own native land.

The prince didn't want his bride to be sad, so he ordered that the hills around the palace should be planted with trees that bore white blossom. Each Spring when the trees came into flower, the hills looked as white as snow, and when the princess looked from her window, the sight that met her was a lovely reminder of the homeland she had left behind, a token of love from a devoted husband.

WEDNESDAY—MARCH 13.

WHEN the members of Digswell Women's Institute saw the surroundings of their local station Welwyn North, they were dismayed; for it was flanked by an untidy, overgrown embankment covered with litter — a complete eyesore.

Being practical ladies they decided they would like to do something about it, so with the approval of British Rail, they raised £1,000 and started their clean-up. The area was completely transformed, planted with shrubs and flowers, and when it became a place of beauty, people stopped dropping litter.

What pleasure the station must have given commuters waiting to go to work each morning, and how it would warm their hearts to realise that people they probably didn't know, cared sufficiently about them to give them a cheerful send-off each day.

THURSDAY—MARCH 14.

IT always makes me feel sad when I hear an elderly person regret the passing of youth. Nowadays, with people living longer, labour-saving appliances and the many opportunities to use retirement creatively, it seems a great pity not to enjoy life to the full instead of wasting time in regrets.

When he was 75, Bishop Willis of Uganda was asked if he would like to have his life over again.

"Why should I?" he replied. "When I have nearly reached the top of the hill with a wonderful prospect before me, why should I want to go back to the bottom again?"

As somebody else once said: "He that knows how to go out to some good purpose and come back in peace can be said to know the secret of happy and successful living."

UNDERSTANDING

WHEN I thought
*   This shouldn't happen to me,*
When I said,
*   "This couldn't happen to me,"*
He opened my eyes to let me see
That He needed someone —
He needed me,
And I thanked the Lord
*   That it happened to me.*

D.J. Morris.

THEY are more important than politicians, and worth far more than the richest business tycoons. Who are they? Mothers, of course!

There is a Jewish proverb: "God could not be everywhere and so he made mothers."

An anonymous, but wise writer is also quoted as saying: "A mother is a person who, if she is not there when you get home from school, you wouldn't know how to get your dinner, and you wouldn't feel like eating it anyway!"

God bless all mothers, whether they be mothers of youngsters or of much more mature "children"!

AFTER these things the word of the Lord came unto Abram in a vision, saying, Fear not, Abram: I am thy shield, and thy exceeding great reward.

Genesis 15:1

THE FRIENDSHIP BOOK

THERE are plenty of poems in praise of roses and daffodils, but Phyllis Ellison has written one about a much humbler little flower:

A glorious mass of yellow,
  They filled the grassy bank,
I thought that they were daffodils,
  But found them lesser rank.
A gardener wouldn't call them flowers,
  These weeds he'd soon send packing,
Yet how bare our country lanes,
  If dandelions were lacking!

AFTER Maureen and Bill were married they moved into a house in a city suburb. I knew they loved their new home, but they were finding it difficult to get to know other people in the street. Nobody seemed to want to speak to them, and everyone remained a stranger.

Then Maureen had a baby and everything changed. "From the first day I went out with the pram all the neighbours stopped to peer under the canopy. They couldn't be more friendly now and we're really getting to know them all.

"I realise now," she went on, "that they wanted to speak to us all the time, but just didn't know what to say."

It's so often like that, isn't it? What we mistake for standoffishness is just plain old-fashioned shyness. Often people are just waiting for an excuse to hold out the hand of friendship.

If there's someone *you've* been thinking of speaking to, do it today — whether or not they have a baby to admire!

SPRING SERENADE

THE FRIENDSHIP BOOK

OVER 800 years ago, St Bernard of Clairvaux asked: "Do you know what piety is? It is leaving time for consideration."

A visitor to Iraq some years ago met the principal of a teachers' training school, who suggested that it would be courteous to call on the Quaimaquam before he left. The Quaimaquam is the name given to the head man of the village; he was obviously interested in all aspects of education, and talked with his visitor for a good couple of hours.

When his guest rose to leave, the Quaimaquam gently took his hands in his own, and gave his parting blessing: "God grant you a safe journey, and may you always have time for consideration."

It's worth thinking about, isn't it, when we are bewildered by a host of never-ending duties, or tempted to be in just too much of a hurry as we rush around without having time to pause and reflect. May we indeed always have time for consideration.

YOU may have come across these lines before, but they never fail to encourage me whenever I read them:

It's what you do, not what you say,
your watchful children spot;
No sermons, please; your kids can see
how very good you're not.
It's your example shapes young lives,
it's how you act each day;
It's useless saying "don't do that",
if that's the game you play,
I must repeat: it's what you do
that makes them live what's good and true.

D

FRIDAY—MARCH 22.

OUR friend Amy is a professional gardener and also has a large garden of her own to care for.

She showed the Lady of the House around it last Spring, and to her relief and astonishment she found that Amy did not mention one Latin name. Before going inside, she asked her why.

"I love all the old traditional names much better," she replied. "Is there anything more delightful than to imagine pinks, pansies, phlox and roses on a cold Winter's day? Latin names can't conjure up the same picture for me. Friends give me plants, too, so in my mind I remember them by the names of my friends. I know it's all rather foolish — don't tell Francis, will you?"

"Of course I will," replied the Lady of the House. "It isn't silly at all. It is a beautiful thought, a unique and lovely way of remembering your friends."

Truly, friendship has its own language.

SATURDAY—MARCH 23.

HERE are the thoughts of one famous man on friendship. Benjamin Disraeli, the Victorian Prime Minister, statesman and novelist, said while addressing the House of Commons, "Friendship is the gift of the gods, and the most precious boon to man."

It is wonderful to have a talent for and an appreciation of that "precious boon", don't you think?

SUNDAY—MARCH 24.

IT was meet that we should make merry, and be glad: for this thy brother was dead, and is alive again; and was lost, and is found.

Luke 15:32

THE FRIENDSHIP BOOK

"THEY also serve who only stand and wait" is one of the fine lines of poetry written by John Milton.

I was reminded of this quotation when I read some memories of the novelist Bernice Rubens, who remembered "terrible Sundays" as a child when she dreaded the arrival of guests. They would be entertained by an elder brother who played the piano and another who performed well on the violin. Bernice could only sit and feel completely inadequate.

Then, one Sunday, her mother told her, "In a family like ours we have to have one listener." That gave her daughter a great gift — the art of listening. This was a lesson she was very grateful for eventually; the ability to listen is a great asset for a novelist.

Those Sundays were not so terrible after all.

I FOUND this little thought in a very unexpected place. It had been left at the bottom of a wire shopping basket in a supermarket, and was written on the back of a shopping list that someone had left behind.

If there be righteousness in every heart,
There will be beauty in every character,
If there be beauty in every character,
There will be harmony in every home,
If there be harmony in every home,
There will be order in every nation,
When there is order in every nation,
There will be peace throughout the world.

Did I say that this is a *little* thought? It is a great thought, and if we all tried hard enough we could help to make it a reality.

THE FRIENDSHIP BOOK

A LITTLE while ago I was re-reading Charles Dickens' tale about Oliver Twist.

Young Oliver fell into the hands of a gang of thieves, comprising the Artful Dodger, the brutal Bill Sykes, and Nancy. When wounded on a burglary expedition, Oliver was rescued by Mrs Maylie and her adopted daughter Rose, who turned out to be Oliver's aunt.

She appears as a young lady, with a gentle, pure spirit and a happy smile. Between them she and Mrs Maylie manage to restore Oliver to health.

In the course of the story, Nancy calls on Rose, and in the presence of Rose's purity and compassion, Nancy bursts into tears and says, "Oh, lady, if there were more like you, there would be fewer like me — there would! Dear lady, why aren't those who claim to be God's own folks as gentle and as kind to us poor wretches as you?"

I am reminded of what someone else once said: "More people are loved and cared into God's Kingdom than are ever preached into it."

GIVE AND TAKE

I WAS only a child,
So how could I know,
You can't have it all,
Because you wish it so,
I had to grow up,
Before I finally knew,
You can't just take,
You must give something, too!

Phyllis Ellison.

LONDON
LIGHTS

FRIDAY—MARCH 29.

AS I expected, my friend Mary was pleased to see me when I called on her recently, one bright and clear Spring afternoon.

"I was hoping you would come," she said, reaching for her "book of treasures", the little notepad she keeps for jotting down anything that especially takes her fancy. "I have found a little prayer that you might like to use for 'The Friendship Book':

For this new morning and its light,
For rest and shelter of the night,
For health and food, for love and friends,
For every gift your goodness sends,
We thank you, gracious Lord.

"I'm glad you like it, too, Francis," said Mary as I copied it down. "It's one I particularly like to say — and I always find that whenever I start the morning with a prayer of thanks, it keeps me right for the whole day."

SATURDAY—MARCH 30.

STARTED to learn something new? Finding it hard going? Take heart from a proverb I remember my grandmother using: "All things are difficult before they are easy."

So don't be discouraged, things will surely improve.

Accept that challenge now!

SUNDAY—MARCH 31.

O DEATH, where is thy sting? O grave, where is thy victory? The sting of death is sin; and the strength of sin is the law. But thanks be to God, which giveth us the victory through our Lord Jesus Christ.

Corinthians I 15:55-57

APRIL

MONDAY—APRIL 1.

APRIL Fools' Day is a very old tradition and nobody can say with any certainty how it came about. Someone has suggested that it originated to help us to judge a man by how he takes a joke against himself.

Author and playwright J. M. Barrie was modest and humorous, and always ready to tell a story against himself.

He used to relate how one of his admirers gave her friend one of his books. The old lady took such a long time to read it — days, weeks, then a month. When her friend asked how she was getting on with it she would say, "It's dreary, weary, uphill work, but I've wrestled through with tougher jobs in my time, and please God I'll wrestle through with this one!"

I am sure that J. M. Barrie would have passed the April Fools' Day test. Only a great man would have repeated a story like that!

TUESDAY—APRIL 2.

I HAD to chuckle at the story I heard about Russell who had become tired of going to Sunday school and said he didn't want to go any more. His parents had both tried to persuade him to return, as had his aunt but without success.

"I'll have a little talk with him," offered Grandma.

"You know, you really ought to go to Sunday school, Russell," she said. "If you don't, Jesus will be very disappointed."

"Oh, no, he won't," came the prompt reply, "because *He* doesn't go there, either!"

THE FRIENDSHIP BOOK

WHEN Oscar Hammerstein II and Richard Rodgers decided to collaborate, the result was a 20-year period when they gave us some of the best musicals ever to appear on stage and screen. They are remembered for spectacles such as "Oklahoma!", "Carousel", "South Pacific", "The King and I" and the ever-popular "Sound Of Music" which touched the emotions of many of us and whose songs are still so familiar.

Hammerstein was something of a philosopher, too. Writing about his work he said: "I know the world is filled with troubles and many injustices, but reality is as beautiful as it is ugly. I think it is just as important to sing about beautiful mornings as it is to talk about the slums. I just couldn't write anything without hope in it."

I'll second that!

CHRISTINA ROSSETTI, the Victorian writer and poet, wrote in her "Easter Carol":

Spring bursts today
For Christ is risen and all the earth's at play.

While Henry Wadsworth Longfellow, the American creator of the well-known poem "Hiawatha", wrote in "The Spanish Student":

'Twas Easter Sunday. The full blossomed trees filled all the air with fragrance and with joy.

Four lines — about new life in its spiritual and natural aspects — which together express the very essence of Easter, wouldn't you agree?

THE FRIENDSHIP BOOK

WHAT a variety of thoughts the word "day" conjures up! My dictionary defines it as a period of 24 hours reckoned from one midnight to the next, or the period of light from sunrise to sunset, or the part of a day occupied with regular activity, especially work.

In addition, there are references to "call it a day", "every dog has his day", "that will be the day", signifying that it is most unlikely to happen, and "at the end of the day", the final reckoning.

On the subject of days, the comedian Terry Scott said, "I live with a fond eye on the past and a shrewd eye on the future. I live for this very moment," while this thoughtful comment came from an old lady's storehouse of sayings:

"There are only three days in the week — yesterday which is gone and done with and can't be changed; today for living now; and tomorrow which will come in time and is full of mystery."

So here's to those three special days — yesterday with all its memories, today with its possibilities, and tomorrow with all its promise.

SPELLING IT OUT

E is for eggs I will paint colours gay,
A is for anthem we'll sing out today;
S is for snowdrops, so white and so pure,
T's for our thanks that will always endure;
E is for ending, the passing of Lent,
R's for rejoice in the victory God sent!

Maurice Fleming.

THE FRIENDSHIP BOOK

AND when Jesus had cried with a loud voice, he said, Father, into thy hands I commend my spirit; and having said thus, he gave up the ghost.

Luke 23:46

"THAT'LL cheer you all up come Easter!" the gardener said after he planted crocus bulbs on the lawn in front of the eventide home where he works.

How the residents looked forward to seeing them coming up, and what a lovely surprise when they saw what he had done! There on the lawn in front of the lounge windows, "written" in glorious orange and mauve crocuses, were two words:

HAPPY EASTER!

I AM sure that you will agree with the poet Robert Browning when you read this verse:

I walked a mile with Pleasure, she chatted all the way,
  But left me none the wiser for all she had to say.
I walked a mile with Sorrow, and ne'er a word said she,
  But oh, the things I learned from her,
When Sorrow walked with me.

We all enjoy and remember moments of pleasure and happiness, yet if we think about it seriously, like Robert Browning, we must surely admit that it is the "sorrows" that enable us to be more mature, sympathetic and loving to others — if we are ready to learn from them.

THE FRIENDSHIP BOOK

I WAS glad to see blackbirds nesting again at the bottom of the garden. They give me enormous pleasure with their nest-building and later, the tender care of their offspring.

As so often happens in families, there is always one chick more venturesome than the others — and one day last year a small fledgling fell to the ground. It was nowhere ready to fly, and within seconds its parents flew to the rescue. One of the birds poked its beak below the small chick, gradually half-lifting and half-pushing it on to the back of the other parent. There, nestled securely, the chick was flown back to the safety of the nest.

Afterwards, excited twitterings came from the nest for a couple of minutes, then suddenly there was silence, and a sense of contented peace.

A welcome reminder from nature that we all need to help each other in so many ways throughout life.

WHENEVER Ethel comes to see us, I have to be on my best behaviour. I must confess she is not exactly the easiest person to get on with — she always seems to be grumbling about something.

She is the sort of person who thinks that young people are all selfish and have no consideration for others. On the other hand, she does not hit it off any better with her own generation — there is, unfailingly, something to displease her about what they say and do.

In fact, there is just no pleasing her. I told her recently that she mustn't judge the jam by the label on the jar. It could be wrongly labelled or it could even be the right one, despite everything, and if she tried it she might find that it is to her taste, after all.

YOU'LL FIND ME
IN THE GARDEN

THE FRIENDSHIP BOOK

DO you remember reading about the Verger of St Mark's? This character in Somerset Maugham's short story entitled "The Verger" is sacked when someone discovers he can't read or write. A widower, living in a lonely bed-sitter above a newsagent's, he tells his landlady he must leave and why.

Widowed herself, she immediately asks him to help with her shop and he proves such an astute businessman that, eventually, she owns several.

They marry and go to see a bank manager to open a joint account and when the time comes to sign documents, the manager is flabbergasted when told of his new client's handicap.

"With your business acumen," he says, "what might you have become, had you been taught to read and write?"

"The Verger of St Mark's," the contented man replies.

HAVE you ever noticed the wonderful rapport between the very young and the very old? So often they share the magic of simple things which the rest of us miss.

I knew a lady in her nineties who was very fond of her great-great-niece. She once remarked that whenever the little girl arrived, the sun came out!

What a lovely memory for that young lady, now grown up with children of her own, to keep in mind for life.

If we could share the wonder of childhood and the wisdom of age more often, the world would be a happier place.

SUNDAY—APRIL 14.

ELECT according to the foreknowledge of God the Father, through sanctification of the Spirit, unto obedience and sprinkling of the blood of Jesus Christ: Grace unto you, and peace, be multiplied.

Peter I 1:2

MONDAY—APRIL 15.

OLD Mr Findlay's family was surprised when he requested a map for his 88th birthday. He lives in the south of England and the map he wanted was of his native Highland county in Scotland. Of what use would it be to him? He's very frail now and it is unlikely that he will ever go there again.

Since he got the map, however, he has had endless pleasure from it. He sits poring over it for hours, following the roads and tracks with his finger — and his memory.

"You get a lovely view from there," he'll say, or "I used to fish on that wee loch when I was a boy." You can tell from his eyes that he's back there now, casting his rod.

He's not able to walk much these days, but with that map in front of him the old man can wander for hours over the hills and glens he loves.

TUESDAY—APRIL 16.

A LIFE of contentment . . . it's not all that difficult to attain. Here's how the poet Longfellow described it:

Each morning sees some task begun,
Each evening sees it close,
Something attempted, something done,
Has earned a night's repose.

THE FRIENDSHIP BOOK

HOTCH-POTCH DAY

TODAY the Lord pleased everyone,
He gave us sun and rain,
A gusty wind to blow the clouds,
And the sky was blue again.
It's been a sort of hotch-potch day,
Designed to suit his flock
Whose tastes are just as varied,
As the weather round the clock.
But now the day is over,
Does He look down far below,
And find the world is satisfied?
Well, no — I wanted snow!

Phyllis Ellison.

I VISIT Bob, my old shepherd friend, every year. He is in his eighties now.

His minister once told me how generous Bob is — giving away not only his flowers, vegetables and home-made cakes to those in need, but also the cash he earns by selling shepherds' crooks to visitors who come to his tranquil village each year.

"This money is given to the church," said the minister. "When we are raising funds Bob is always the first to contribute, and this somehow always makes us all give more!"

Later, speaking to Bob about this never-ending generosity he told me, "I've found that the old saying 'The more you give the more you will receive' is true, not in terms of cash, but in terms of new opportunities — and love."

FRIDAY—APRIL 19.

DO YOU REMEMBER?

WHEN I go out or stay with friends
We've memories to share,
The saddest time is going home
And knowing you're not there.
I think of you with each new day
In April or December,
I wish that I could turn to you
And say: "Do you remember?"

We used to talk about the past
And people we had known,
The problems and the happiness
And how the years had flown.
So I will hold those memories
And love's undying ember,
And though I may not hear your voice
I'll know, we both remember.

Iris Hesselden.

SATURDAY—APRIL 20.

WHAT a resounding epitaph to be honoured by: band leader Duke Ellington said of Louis Armstrong, "He was born poor, died rich, and never hurt anyone on the way."

SUNDAY—APRIL 21.

HOW precious also are thy thoughts unto me, O God! how great is the sum of them! If I should count them, they are more in number than the sand: when I awake, I am still with thee.

Psalms 139:17-18

D

GUARDIAN OF THE SEAS

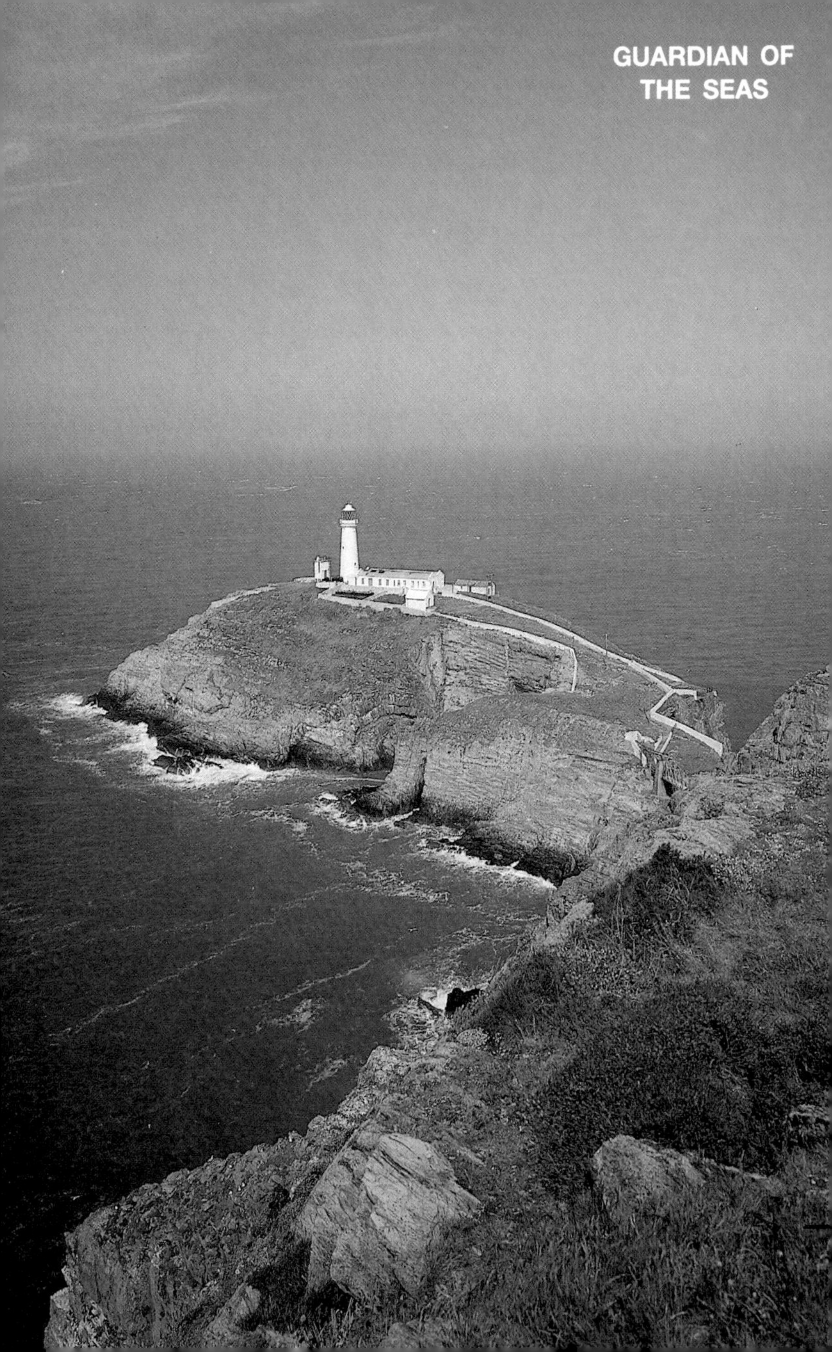

THE FRIENDSHIP BOOK

IN the village church at Copford near Colchester in Essex are some magnificent examples of wall paintings. The church was visited during the 12th century by painters travelling across Europe and they endowed the interior of the church with their work. They are similar to those in Canterbury Cathedral.

When I last visited it, I found some local artists busy working on their own ideas for a wall painting, and inviting people to add their own artistic touches. These sketches were later sold to raise money towards the cost of conserving the church's art work.

As well as establishing a link between 12th and 20th century art and the community, these new paintings have made a contribution to maintaining part of the country's heritage.

It demonstrates that as individuals, our efforts may seem insignificant, but when we all work together there is nothing we cannot do.

JOE used to have a large and beautiful rhododendron bush in his garden, but three years ago he cut it down almost to the roots. It had become too overgrown and some branches had died off.

Last week he called over to me as I passed his house. "Just look at that!" he exclaimed, pointing to where green leaves were sprouting and young shoots springing up from the roots. "You would think," he said, "after the setback it had, that it might never have recovered. Instead, it's starting all over again."

He looked at me. "If I ever feel like giving up on anything, I'm going to come and look at this bush. If *it* can fight back like that, so can *we*."

Indeed we can.

THE FRIENDSHIP BOOK

HANDS — what wonderful tools they are, and they can be used for doing so much good in this world.

How quickly do we react when someone says, "Give us a hand, will you?" Are we ready, without hesitation, to give a hand, or do we thrust our hands in our pockets, so to speak?

Just think for a moment of the hands that have helped you throughout your life — the hands that helped you in your youngest years; the hands that guided you, often unknown to you, through the difficult years of young adulthood; the hands around you that help you now in so many ways. How we rely on many different kinds of hands, and how we tend to take them all for granted!

Next time someone says, "Give us a hand, will you?" let's be ready — and keep those pockets well zipped up.

I LIKE the story of an old lady who was given two identical parrots. She thought one would be male and the other female, but did not know how to tell the difference, so she draped a cloth over the cage and watched them secretly.

She observed for several hours, until one looked round rather nervously, sidled along the perch and gave its companion a quick peck on the cheek.

The male had surely been identified! She whipped off the cloth, caught hold of the parrot and painted a white ring round its neck.

All went well until the minister came for tea.

The parrot called out: "Oh, so they caught you at it, too, did they?"

THE FRIENDSHIP BOOK

HIS PRESENCE

*H*E is here, because you see
I feel him watching over me,

*He is here, and I know
With me everywhere I go.*

*He is here, can you hear him too?
He is waiting to hear from you.*

Carole M. Pickworth.

HAVE you noticed how troubles seem less when you have a friend to confide in? It is good to have a trusted, willing listener to talk to when things are not going too well.

One day I mentioned this to Judith, who is now 90. Sadly, all her close friends are no longer with us, but she reminded me, obviously with great faith, that she still has one Special Friend who listens to her fears and watches over her all the time.

How comforting it was to be reminded that we are never friendless and that we can always trust a higher power so completely with our lives.

AND Samuel said to all the people, See ye him the Lord hath chosen, that there is none like him among all the people? And all the people shouted, and said, God save the king.

Samuel I 10:24

I ONCE remember a hospital doctor saying that patients recover more quickly if they are able to look out on a tree, rather than a blank wall. Likewise, housewives who are unable to look out over a garden while they do their household chores, often like to have a row of colourful plants on the kitchen window-sill. There's no doubt that to have beauty and colour around us is a great lifter of spirits.

In her lovely novel "The Herb of Grace", Elizabeth Goudge wrote of the young heroine Sally: "Though her head was aching . . . she could think of nice things — the Cumberland Hills, the lambs, her nanny, who had taught her this trick of detachment. 'When you're sick or sorry, child,' she had said, 'think of other things as much as you are able. It's just practice. Start young and you'll soon get the trick of it.' And most astonishingly . . . she fell asleep."

It's a habit we might all find helpful to cultivate!

I N my bookcase I came across a well-thumbed copy of one of the "Just William" books.

What a mischievous urchin William is, and what a contrast to his creator. Richmal Crompton was a studious, serious-minded lady whose first choice of profession was teaching. However, an attack of polio left her partially paralysed and compelled her to abandon this to become a full-time writer.

I suspect there is a bit of the rebel and adventurer in all of us, and possibly Richmal got this out of her system by writing about William. One book was entitled "William The Conqueror". Richmal was also a conqueror, bravely surmounting her disability and delighting thousands of readers. How lucky for us!

MAY

FATHER, FORGIVE ME

FORGIVE me, Father, I have failed,
I've been downhearted and depressed,
I didn't see the birds today,
Or notice how the trees were dressed.
Things didn't seem to go my way,
I felt disgruntled and dismayed,
I magnified my aches and pains
Until I felt a bit afraid.
Then suddenly I felt You near,
Your blessings were so clear to see,
Forgive me, Father, when I fail,
For You, I know, will not fail me.

Iris Hesselden.

IF you are an animal lover you will know the pleasure it gives to your pets just to be touched — a dog trembles with delight when you stroke its middle; a cat purrs when rubbed on top of its head; a pony responds warmly when its neck is patted.

Well, we are the very same as these animals, you know. The touch of a loved one is just as important to us, as humans, as it is to our pets. Yet in the busy, bustling lives we live, it is so easy to forget this all-important aspect of human love, isn't it?

So, next time you feel the urge to hold hands with your loved one — do so. Never mind what other people think, or if they stare!

IN PASTURES GREEN

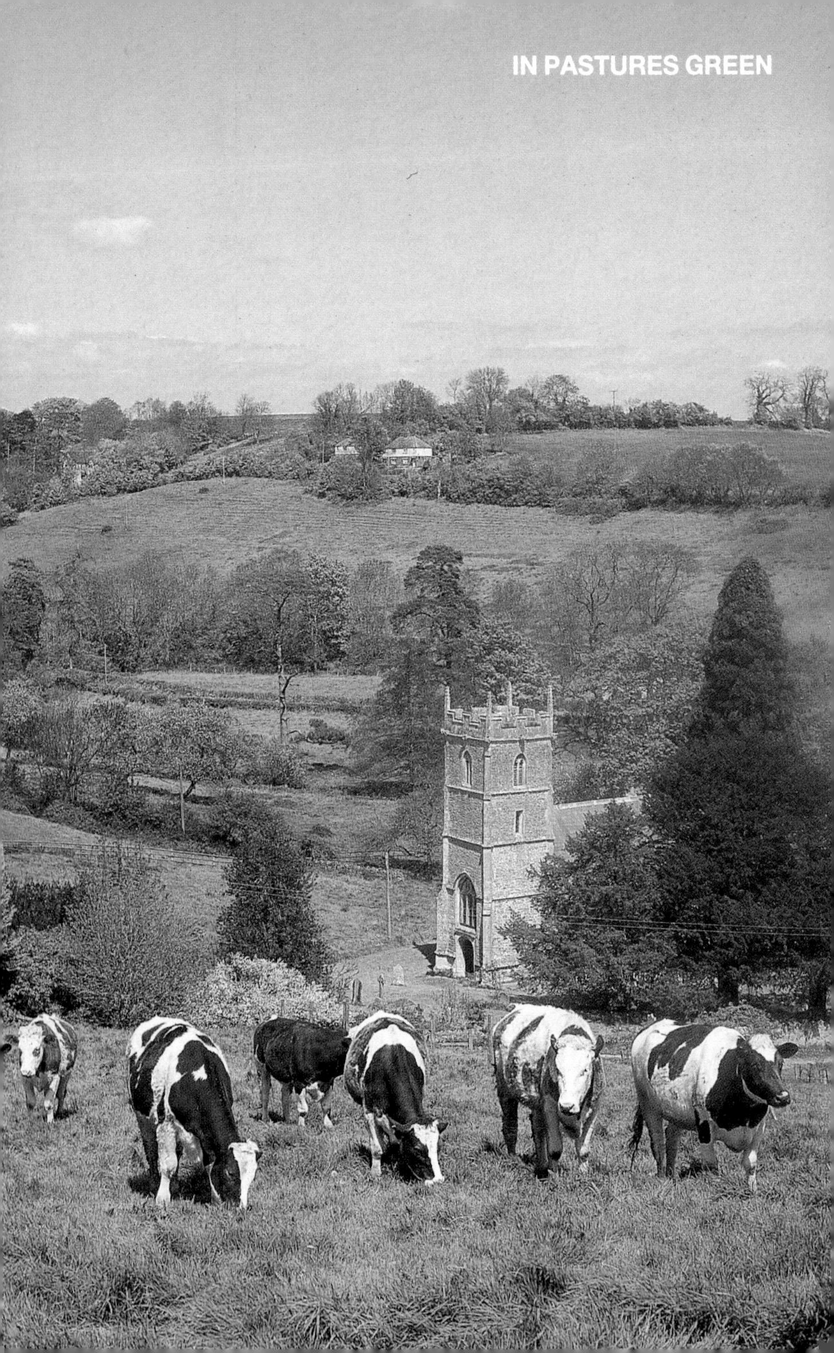

FRIDAY—MAY 3.

SOMETIMES I feel sorry for young folk. They are constantly being told about: "The way things *used* to be."

They're reminded how lucky they are to have so many possessions, so much freedom, so many holidays, and so on. However, what kind of an example should older people set them? How often have youngsters been given the wrong advice or instilled the wrong values?

We have a beautiful world to treasure and a great deal to share, if we can only find the way. I think George Bernard Shaw had the right idea, and I like his words: "Life is not meant to be easy, my child; but take courage, it can be delightful!"

SATURDAY—MAY 4.

A TOURIST had reached a small town where he intended to spend the night before travelling farther. He joined several men who were sitting together at the porch in front of the general store.

They seemed a taciturn bunch, and after several abortive attempts to join the conversation, the visitor said, "Is there a law against talking here?"

"No *law* against it," grunted one of his companions, "but there's an understanding that no one's to speak unless he's sure he can improve on silence."

He'd got something there, hadn't he?

SUNDAY—MAY 5.

WAIT on the Lord: be of good courage, and he shall strengthen thine heart: wait, I say, on the Lord.

Psalms 27:14

THE FRIENDSHIP BOOK

WHAT exactly is wealth? I remember reading an article by Christopher Brasher about a visit to Fair Isle. He met Anne Sinclair who, with her husband Barry, tended a 19-acre croft; there they brought up their two children, both now grown up.

Anne told him, "We are rich now." She was not thinking of money, but in terms of a way of life. She went on, "What we have here is time. We are a discussion household, there are no commands, but instead agreement. All you can do is to give children the basic values, teach them to care about other people. I have only two rules: that intolerance is a dreadful thing and that thou shall not bear false witness. My mother always had time for me and I am pleased that my children always have so much time for her. As soon as Steven comes home to the island from college, he takes his granny for a walk."

Yes, there are no riches like family life.

I LOVE words that are onomatopoeic. You know the sort of thing — they sound like the noise or action they describe. I enjoy the round wetness of the word "plop," the exhilaration of "whoosh" and "whiz" and the jolly, Christmassy ring to "jingle".

Some words, of course, have a definitely less-pleasing tone. "Grudge" sounds to me exactly like the heavy, dragging burden it usually is, while "vindictive" and "spiteful" seem to contain a sharp, spiky sound that echoes their meaning. How much nicer are the sounds of "chuckle" and "trill"!

Beware, though, for once you start looking for words that sound like their meanings, you may find the hobby addictive!

THE FRIENDSHIP BOOK

HERE are some more items from my collection of "Points To Ponder" which you might like to think about at the start of another day.

You can't build up a reputation on what you are *going* to do.

Our problems are the tools God uses to polish us, not demolish us.   (Mel Tari)

There's no problem in the world that can't be overcome with a little ingenuity.   (St Augustine)

The more we count the blessings we have, the less we crave the luxuries we haven't.   (William A. Ward)

ONE of our young friends, Lucy, is a talented clarinetist and when she was chosen to play a solo in the local youth orchestra, the Lady of the House and I went along to the performance.

After the concert, one of the people in our party remarked to Lucy's mother, "How I enjoyed that, and how lucky Lucy is to be able to play so beautifully." Lucy's mother looked thoughtful for a moment, then said, "Yes, I suppose she is lucky to have been given such a talent. Her high standard, though, wasn't achieved without a great deal of hard work."

It's true of so many things besides music. As the saying goes, "Luck is what happens when preparation meets opportunity." It's surprising what we are able to do once we have set our mind to it. Like a bunch of keys, we've got to find the one that opens our particular door.

THE FRIENDSHIP BOOK

WE live in a world of rapid change, it's true, and yet it's amazing how many things of beauty which inspired the great poets of yesterday can still be enjoyed today.

When Shelley wrote: "Hail to thee, blithe spirit! Bird thou never wert", he was listening to the same song of the skylark as we can hear in the countryside now.

In Spring the cuckoo calls again and again as he did when Wordsworth wrote:
O blithe newcomer! I have heard,
I hear thee and rejoice.

Robert Burns' "wee modest crimson-tipped flow'r" — the humble daisy — brightens many a lawn (whether it's wanted or not!), and there are thousands of streams like the one which Tennyson heard saying:
I chatter, chatter, as I flow
To join the brimming river.

As long as all these things are still with us, I don't think the world's such a bad place, do you?

SO CHEERFUL
I SMILE on Sundays — it's a day I like;
I smile on Mondays, as I ride my bike;
I smile on Tuesdays, as everyone knows;
I smile on Wednesdays, as the wind blows;
I smile on Thursdays, as I shop in town;
I smile on Fridays — Why wear a frown?
When it rains on Saturdays, I smile then, too;
If you were as happy, so would you!

Shirley E. Peckham.

THE FRIENDSHIP BOOK

TO whom God would make known what is the riches of the glory of this mystery among the Gentiles; which is Christ in you, the hope of glory.

Colossians 1:27

A PARTY of tourists landed on Iona, the peaceful island of St Columba. They were escorted by a guide and as they passed the old chapel he indicated some ancient graves containing the remains of Scots and Norwegian kings.

"There on the right are the old Scots kings, and there on the left . . ." — he pointed to another row of graves — ". . . are the Norwegian ones."

"Just a minute!" exclaimed a rather precise-looking man. "I came on this trip last year and you said then that the ones on the *right* were the Norwegian graves."

"Ach," retorted the guide with a grin, "ye know how it is. Iona's so quiet they sometimes entertain themselves by changing places."

THE Lady of the House had bought a fresh pineapple for a tea-time treat one hot Summer's day, and what a prickly thing it was, too! I watched as she prepared it, cutting through the tough ends and carefully paring off all the sharply-pointed outer skin, until at last the lovely juicy fruit was ready to eat.

It made me think about all those people around us that we have never got to know properly. Perhaps through a naturally reserved nature, or circumstances of life, they are difficult to approach. Yet, with patience, hidden underneath the prickly exterior, we may well discover a personality to surprise and delight us.

THE FRIENDSHIP BOOK

OUR minister recently told us a story about an elderly lady learning to crochet. She didn't see too well, so didn't always notice when she dropped a stitch, but she still enjoyed doing something useful.

Friends gave her all their odd balls of wool, and she chose the most colourful to crochet squares which she eventually stitched together into a blanket. When there was an appeal for blankets to be given to one of the poorer African countries, she gladly donated her colourful one.

In that African country the Christian Aid workers were trying to buy land from the local head man. They wanted to extend their clinic, but the head man refused to negotiate with them.

On the day the parcel arrived, the chief was among those present. As the blankets were unpacked, he saw the brightly-coloured crocheted one and told the charity workers that if they would let him have the blanket, he would give them the land they had been asking for.

He walked off proudly with the blanket draped round his shoulders, leaving a very thankful team of helpers. From the best the old lady had managed to do came the gift of the land for the clinic.

In the words of the hymn writer, William Cowper: "God moves in a mysterious way His wonders to perform."

I CAME across a beautiful little definition of friendship the other day: "The light of friendship is like phosphorous, seen plainly when all around is dark".

Truly a most encouraging thought.

A MAN'S LOVE

A MAN *kissed his wife five times upon her head,*
As he lay close beside her in the darkness in their
bed,
"The first one is for love so pure and true,
The second for my daughter with her eyes so blue,
The third for my devotion of my love to you,
The fourth for the hard times we have struggled
through."
Yet the fifth kiss was different and lingered on her
hair,
"For this kiss," he said, "is for the years we will share."
                                            Martine Jenkins.

SATURDAY—MAY 18.

I OFTEN dip into Ralph Waldo Emerson's essays, and usually find something fresh that I haven't seen before — or taken in properly. I would like to share this little thought of his with you today: "I like the silent church before the service begins better than any preaching."

Prayers, a sermon or a hymn can strengthen our faith, but silence — complete and utter silence — can be infinitely comforting, too.

SUNDAY—MAY 19.

I HAVE set the Lord always before me: because he is at my right hand, I shall not be moved. Therefore my heart is glad, and my glory rejoiceth: my flesh also shall rest in hope.

                                            Psalms 16:8-9

THE FRIENDSHIP BOOK

SHORTLY before retiring as Archbishop of Canterbury, Robert Runcie initiated the Church Urban Fund — Faith in the City. Its aim was that by regular and often self-sacrificing giving by church members in relatively better-off areas, projects could be set up to tackle problems in areas of need where there was little money. It was a direct response to the command to love our neighbour as ourself.

St Martin's Church in Wolverhampton is surrounded by a large piece of land, previously used for tipping rubbish. Through grants from the Church Urban Fund, and others, the grounds have now been transformed. One hundred and twenty skips of rubbish were removed free of charge by the council and a new fence put an end to dumping.

The main work of restoration and turfing was done by trainees, then a team of volunteers moved in to build a Nature Trail with pool and shrubs. An adventure playground and safe toddlers' area with a sandpit was also made.

The grounds have been much in use for Holiday Clubs, uniformed organisations, Mothers and Toddlers, and in nice weather the Pensioners' Luncheon Club and Coffee Morning meet outdoors.

Now the once-derelict site is a real asset to the area and neighbours have expressed appreciation of the improvements. It all goes to prove that with hard work, cooperation and a desire to help others, a great deal can be done to find the best in an uncompromising situation.

PEOPLE who really want to do something find a way — the others find an excuse.

F

THE FRIENDSHIP BOOK

MRS S. BALLET of Shaftsbury, Dorset, sent me
this delightful poem. It's addressed to a grand-
child who seems to be more than slightly mischievous!

There's jam on your nose —
And cream in your hair!
There's egg on your chin —
How did it get there?

You smell very strongly
Of Mummy's best scent!
You're covered in lipstick —
So THAT'S where it went!

There's cake in the bath —
And what's this down the loo?
An apple — a hairbrush —
A teddy — a SHOE!

I know that we said
The cat likes to be clean —
But you MUSTN'T put Puss
In the washing machine!

You climb on my knee —
Put your arms round my neck!
Your kiss is so sweet —
Oh well — what the heck!

I COMMEND the definition of an acrobat, which
Mrs Taylor from Consett told me:

"Someone who will do a good turn — and bend
over backwards to help you."

The least supple of us can manage to be *that* kind
of acrobat.

FRIDAY—MAY 24.

OUR churches are full of fascinating little bits of history — fine alabaster effigies of the famous, stained glass windows in gratitude for someone's life, and monuments commemorating faithful service to a church. Something unique in my experience was the modest brass plate on the wall of the church in the tiny village of Hamstall Ridware:

Pupils and Staff of Pipewood School
Evacuated from Birmingham
Worshipped here 1940-1945.
With grateful thanks.

What a depth of meaning in those few words. I can only guess the feelings of war-time parents knowing that their children had been received and welcomed into a safe community in rural England.

"I was a stranger, and ye took me in."

SATURDAY—MAY 25.

IF we refer to somebody as a gossip, we usually mean that the person habitually talks about others, especially in a malicious way.

Now, did you know that the world originally was "Godsyb" and stood for the specially chosen female friend asked to stand beside you at your child's baptism? She was someone highly regarded, trusted and to be depended upon.

There's a lot to be said for a bit of gossip done at the right time and in the right way. It can restore harmony, correct a wrong impression about somebody and boost their morale. So, if I am ever tempted to indulge in a bit of gossip, I'm resolved to remember what it once stood for.

THE FRIENDSHIP BOOK

YE are the light of the world. A city that is set on an hill cannot be hid. Neither do men light a candle, and put it under a bushel, but on a candlestick; and it giveth light unto all that are in the house. Let your light so shine before men, that they may see your good works and glorify your Father which is in heaven.

Matthew 5:14-16

MONDAY—MAY 27.

OUR young friend Liz tells me that she has three eyes. Let me explain. Liz is from Shetland and was brought up on a small, peaceful island there. Now, still in her teens, she is attending college in the heart of London. What a change in lifestyle! How does she cope? Well, that's where her "third eye" comes in.

She wrote to me: "I was very lost and unhappy at first. The evenings were the worst, but now I have found a way to fight the feeling. When I'm walking back to my flat at the end of the day I don't see the shops and buildings. In my mind's eye I see the fields back home, the smoke rising from the houses scattered over the island. I see the cattle grazing and I even meet some of the crofters and they wave to me as I pass.

"So you see, I no longer feel cut off from home. I know that all the people and things I love are still there, and that I will see them all again — and not just with my 'third eye'!"

I am glad to say that, in her latest letter, Liz tells us that she has now started to make friends. Loneliness can be a terrible thing for a young person in strange surroundings. If you know someone like that, tell them about Liz's third eye, and how it helped her through a difficult time.

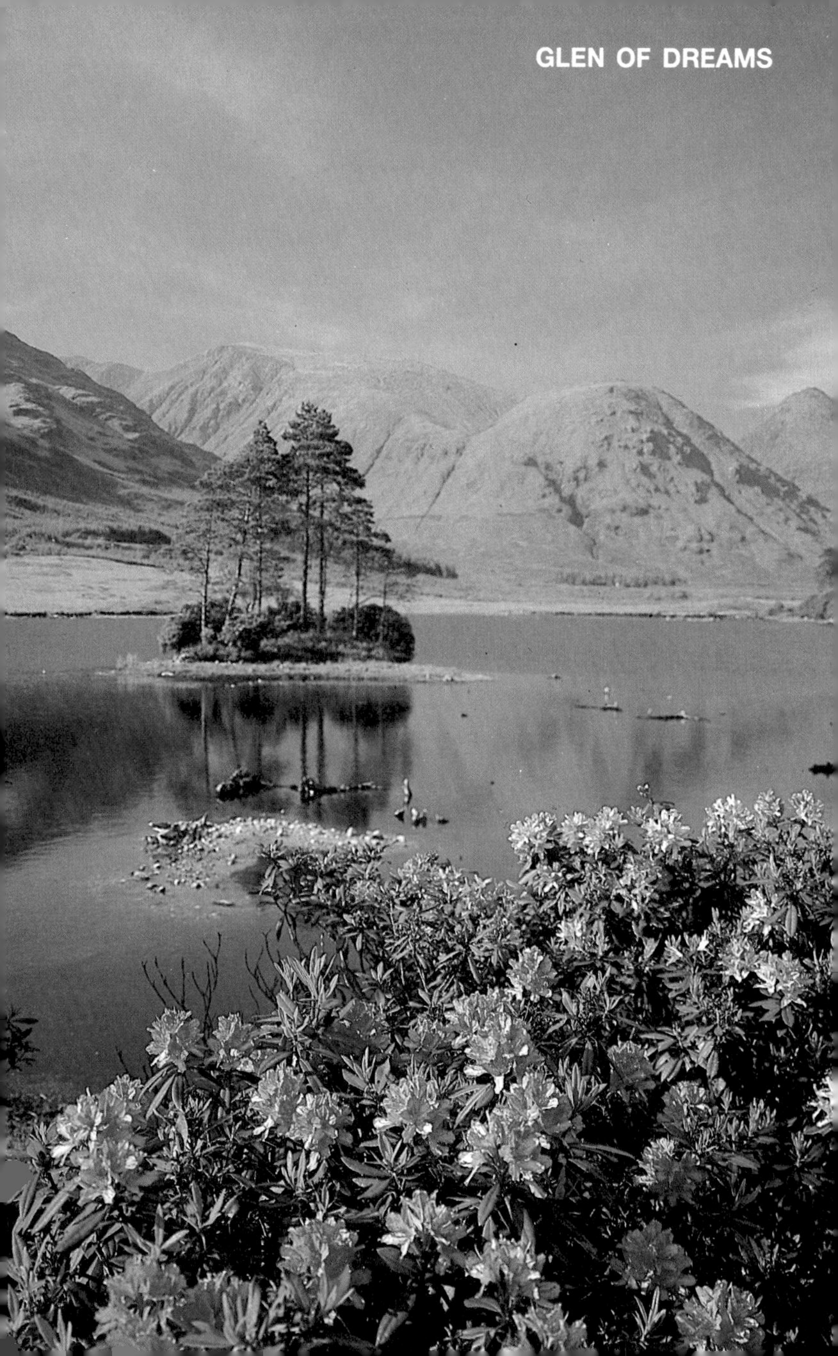

GLEN OF DREAMS

WE were paying one of our regular visits to our friend Mary, and the Lady of the House was telling her all about some work we had just had done in the kitchen and the great amount of mess to be cleaned up when the workmen had departed.

"And what do you think?" said the Lady of the House. "I was filling the bucket to mop the kitchen floor when the phone rang. By the time I came back, the water had overflowed and the floor was awash with suds."

Instead of the instant sympathy she had expected, Mary said with a twinkle in her eye, "Well, my dear, you did say the floor needed washing and what better way could you have had of giving it a really good clean?"

As I have mentioned before, Mary is something of a philosopher!

WEDNESDAY—MAY 29.

WHEN we were younger we moved house on more than one occasion. Before taking the plunge, we used to look for what we thought were the most important things to make daily living more comfortable — attractive surrounding buildings, good shops, a convenient bus service.

We still know that these things can be very important, but we no longer think of them as the things that matter most. We have learned that the quality of life is influenced most by the *people* with whom we live, rather than by the features of a neighbourhood.

So, wherever we live, may we find friends whose influence will be for good — but above all, may we be such a friend to others.

THE FRIENDSHIP BOOK

THANK YOU

THANK You, Lord, for the seasons
As they swiftly come and go;
For the special days of Summer
And sudden, Winter snow.
Thank You, Lord, for the beauty
Of the distant, misty hills;
For the trees in Springtime glory
And joyful daffodils.
Thank You, Lord, for those I love
And the love they give to me;
For all I've learned, for all I am,
And all I hope to be.
Thank You, Lord, for all my life,
For the laughter, hope and care;
For all the times when You were close —
Accept my "Thank You" prayer.

Iris Hesselden.

A SALES representative once went to a conference and the main speaker began by lighting a candle.

"I want you to make that candle go out," she said to the assembled audience. Everyone sat there trying to get the candle to go out, using sheer will-power — but the flame still burned brightly. Then one member of the audience went up to the stage and simply snuffed out the candle.

The speaker drew breath for a moment, then said, "Yes, you can will things to happen, but sometimes it is no use just sitting there wishing — you have to *do* something about it."

How true — action is what gets things done.

JUNE

SATURDAY—JUNE 1.

"I'M just going to slip round to Michelle's house with this bunch of flowers from our garden," said the Lady of the House one day after tea. Michelle is a young lass who lives in our road and works in the local florist's.

"Well, that's a nice idea," I replied, but the Lady of the House could tell by the expression on my face that I was puzzled.

"I went into the shop this afternoon," she explained, "and I thanked Michelle for arranging my birthday bouquet so nicely and delivering it to the door. She said that she was glad I had liked it and then remarked, rather ruefully I thought, 'I never have flowers to keep for myself. My job is to give them away.' I was so touched that I decided Michelle should have a nice bunch of her own without delay."

It made me reflect on the giving of flowers. They are an accepted token of friendship to the sick or elderly, or to those celebrating an anniversary or retirement, but perhaps we rarely think that someone young would appreciate flowers so much.

However, there's one young lady, not very far away, who had a smile brought to her face that evening — by a bunch of flowers.

SUNDAY—JUNE 2.

GOD is our refuge and strength, a very present help in trouble. Therefore will not we fear, though the earth be removed, and though the mountains be carried into the midst of the sea.

Psalms 46:1-2

THE FRIENDSHIP BOOK

MONDAY—JUNE 3.

AN old Perthshire friend used to make this fine toast: "May the best ye've ever seen be the warst ye'll *ever* see!"

TUESDAY—JUNE 4.

VERONICA used to be an art and craft teacher. When she retired, she found she'd quite a lot of time to spare so she offered her services to a nearby old people's home. Now she goes there each Friday afternoon to help the residents with some simple handicrafts, and how popular her visits are!

Many of Veronica's friends keep an eye open for useful bits and pieces of material, and when we called to see her she was happily sorting out her latest bag of scraps.

"I suppose there will be things there that you won't be able to use," remarked the Lady of the House, as she surveyed the array of coloured material.

"On the contrary," said Veronica, "I shall be able to find a use for every donation. These old curtains will make lovely shoe bags — one for every new child in the school — and the skirts will be cut into strips to make strings for the bags. Then look at this pretty flowered material and these scraps of velvet, lace and brocade. I shall put them into my collage bag and they will be ideal for the ladies to use for their pictures."

The Lady of the House was thoughtful as we walked home. "Veronica certainly puts into practice the principle of making the best of what she has been given," she said.

"Don't you think there's a moral in her scrap bag, Francis — and that it's something we ought to apply in life as well as just needlework?"

THE FRIENDSHIP BOOK

I WONDER how many people still treasure the Lord Wharton Bible they won in their schooldays?

Philip, Lord Wharton, who died 300 years ago this year, was a deeply religious man. His will provided for the establishment of a trust to distribute free Bibles to young people, and the charity still provides up to 1500 copies each year.

They are intended for young people who are members of a church or Sunday school, and the applicant is expected to be able to recite by heart at least five verses of the Bible, as well as showing an understanding of certain selected passages.

It is good to know that help has been given towards the physical needs of people by benefactors in the past. However, in an age when moral values appear to be declining, it is just as important that the spiritual lives of young people are safeguarded, too. That's why I remember with gratitude Philip, Lord Wharton, and all he did to help to build good foundations for life.

MANY years ago — *too* many! — I spent a happy week camping with other lads in my Scout troop. We had been out one day and it was completely dark when we walked back up the field to our tents.

Then one of the boys pointed excitedly to the sky. He had spotted the Milky Way, something he had never noted before, myriad twinkling stars stretched across the sky. It was a wonderful sight and something we never forgot.

Years later, as I reflected on that experience, it seemed to me that often when skies are at their darkest for us, it is then that we are able to see the stars most clearly.

THE FRIENDSHIP BOOK

GOD SHOWS IN YOUR FACE

YOU don't have to tell how you live every day;
You don't have to say if you work or you pray,
A tried true barometer serves in the place,
However you live, it will show in your face.

The false, the deceit that you bear in your heart,
Will not stay inside where it first got a start,
For sinew and blood are a thin veil of lace,
What you wear in your heart, you will wear in your face.

If your life is unselfish, if for others you live,
For not what you get, but how much you can give,
If you live close to God in His infinite Grace,
You don't have to tell it, it shows in your face.

                                                    Anon.

AS you know, the Lady of the House and I love discussing our favourite words. She says she likes "tranquillity" because it sounds so soothing and relaxing. "Eternal", with its soft opening vowel sound and depth of meaning is another special word.

I favour an all-time favourite: "serendipity". My dictionary defines this word as "the faculty of making happy and unexpected discoveries by accident."

We end our chats on a happy note, for if we find tranquillity, our lives will be more peaceful. Then love, as we know and believe, is eternal.

If we have a little serendipity, there will always be a touch of enchantment in the world.

THE FRIENDSHIP BOOK

I AM the good shepherd: the good shepherd giveth his life for the sheep.

John 10:11

ONE way of being cheerful is to heed the apocryphal Beatitude: "Blessed is he who can laugh at himself. He has endless amusement."

HOW I love the month of June "When the bee is on the wing and on the clustering hazel boughs, the linnets sit and sing." It's the time of roses and wedding bells; garden fêtes and barbecues; long, sunny days and warm evenings when I can linger in the garden far into the evening.

It's the month, too, when we commemorate St Barnabas whose day is on the 11th June. Before the calendar was changed in Britain in 1752 it was also the longest day of the year — "Barnaby bright, all day and no night." Special decorations were put up and haymaking began, for the old country motto advised "By St Barnabas, put scythe to grass." That is why St Barnabas is often shown in pictures carrying a hay rake.

Matthew Arnold described this time of year beautifully:

Soon will the high midsummer pomps come on,
Soon will the musk carnations break and swell,
Soon we shall have gold-dusted snapdragon,
Sweet William with its homely cottage smell
And stocks in fragrant blow.

QUIET WATERS

THE FRIENDSHIP BOOK

I CAME across an interesting story about some village sportsmen. The football squad was especially good and everyone was very proud of it. The cricket team was different — after having difficulty getting a team together at all, they found that they'd eleven good bowlers and no batsmen!

It occurred to me how uninteresting life would be, if, like the cricket team, we were all blessed with the same talents.

It is the diversity of gifts amongst people that makes for part of life's richness — and for this we should be thankful.

I HAVE heard and read many versions of grace, prayers offered before meals. This one was sent to me from Yorkshire:

We thank Thee, Lord, for common food,
For trotters, tripe, pig's cheek,
For steak and onions, with their crude
But appetising reek.
Potatoes in their jackets make
Us plain folk honour Thee;
And thou art with us when we bake
Fresh shrimps for Sunday tea.

Thy people's praise is overdue
But see, dear Lord, we kneel
To offer thanks for Irish stew
And tasty, cheap cowheel.
Now wait a minute, Lord! Don't miss
The last word on our lips;
We thank thee most of all for this,
Thy gift of fish and chips.

THE FRIENDSHIP BOOK

HAVE you heard the story of the small boy who, becoming tired of his toys, went and asked his father for something new to do. Dad was busy sorting through some books and papers and was puzzled for the moment what to suggest. Then he happened to turn the pages of an old magazine and found a map of the world printed on one side of a page. This gave him an idea — tearing it out, he then cut it into many-shaped pieces, like a jigsaw, and throwing them down on the hearthrug said, "There you are, son, piece this map together again."

Within a few minutes a small voice announced, "Look, Daddy, I've fixed it."

His father was amazed. "How did you manage it so quickly?" he asked.

"Well, you see, on the other side is the face of a man, and I knew if I put him together all right, I should put the world right, too."

JAMES was once a music teacher and church organist, and also composed songs for school concerts every year. He produced musicals for his local operatic society and took part in the Gilbert and Sullivan productions himself. He was always so unassuming about his hard work, and more often than not was overlooked when votes of thanks were being said.

He is 90 now, and still busy — he told me that he is composing an opera.

"How do you get through all the work, James?" I asked, secretly envying his energy and enthusiasm.

"I never wonder *when* to do a thing, Francis — I just do it *now*," were his parting words, as he hurried away, waving cheerfully.

SUNDAY—JUNE 16.

THOU shalt not avenge, nor bear any grudge against the children of thy people, but thou shalt love thy neighbour as thyself: I am the Lord.

Leviticus 19:18

MONDAY—JUNE 17.

MOLLY had just returned from spending a few days at the seaside. The break had been much needed, but it was the first time she had been away since being widowed, and she was understandably a little apprehensive about going alone.

Her friends' thoughts were with her while she was away, and after a week of dreadful weather, they were half-expecting her return to be a dismal one.

To their surprise, though, when they began to offer commiserations, she smiled.

"I must admit," she said, "that at first I thought it was going to be dreadful. The rain poured, the gales howled, and I began to feel really disheartened at the thought of spending the whole holiday stuck in the boarding-house. Then I realised that all the other guests were in the same situation, and I soon found myself enjoying long chats, and joining in games. In fact, I had such a good time that next year I'm positively hoping for bad weather!"

The dark clouds really did have a silver lining!

TUESDAY—JUNE 18.

THESE words by Thomas Carlyle are as true today as when they were first written, last century:

"The greatest of faults, I should say, is to be conscious of none."

THE FRIENDSHIP BOOK

"THAT'S what I call togetherness," remarked a passing neighbour one sunny morning.

The remark was prompted by the sight of the Lady of the House and myself sitting companionably side by side painting the garden fence with wood preservative. It was a pleasant day for such a task and the time passed quickly.

I was reminded of something I heard about Rawicz and Landauer, who played simultaneously on two pianos and were very popular with their audiences some years ago. It is said they had such rapport that even if they were practising in separate rooms, they could still keep together.

Whether it be at work or at leisure, if we have a companion with whom we are completely "in tune", how fortunate we are.

THURSDAY—JUNE 20.

PRIDE. It's a funny sort of quality, isn't it? Too much may be bad, but too little can be a disadvantage. For example, Bob is a perfectly adequate handyman, yet never offers to help his neighbours because he has no faith in his workmanship.

Annie, a wonderful cook, only rarely asks people to share a meal, and then spoils the occasion by constant unnecessary apologies for its "poor" quality. Both are nice people, but by refusing to take any pride in their skills, they deprive others of help, and themselves of friendship.

As for me, I like to remember the words of an old friend: "Pride is like sugar," he said. "Too much is hard to swallow, but stir in just a little, and you'll find it sweetens everything!"

G

FRIDAY—JUNE 21.

OUR friend Mary was sitting in a deckchair reading a magazine one glorious day when the Lady of the House and I called.

"I've been reading about that lovely film actress, Audrey Hepburn," she told us. "How beautiful she was! I'll always remember her dressed in splendour for the Ball, as Eliza Doolittle in 'My Fair Lady'.

"But did you know the reason why she devoted the latter part of her life to being an ambassador for the UNICEF cause? It was because she had been a deprived child, living in war-torn Amsterdam and, at times, had only tulip bulbs or endives to eat. As a result, she felt she could do this work, having something in common with the world's hungry children."

On hearing of her death, another well-known Hollywood actress expressed the thought:

"God has gained another angel today."

"Surely," said Mary, "a lovely tribute to someone who not only looked like an angel, but *was* one, too."

SATURDAY—JUNE 22.

MY friend peers in on me with merry
Wise face, and though the sky stay dim,
The very light of day, the very
Sun's self comes with him.
                    Algernon Charles Swinburne.

SUNDAY—JUNE 23.

FOR ye were as sheep going astray; but are now returned unto the Shepherd and Bishop of your souls.

                    Peter I 2:25

THE FRIENDSHIP BOOK

MONDAY—JUNE 24.

THE cowslips that once bloomed so profusely in the hedgerows are rarely seen today, perhaps because they were over-picked in days gone by when homemade cowslip wine was so popular.

In May 1906, Edith Holden, in her beautifully illustrated "Country Diary" recalls picking her first bunch of cowslips of the year; and in the 1870s when the Rev. Francis Kilvert visited his country parishioners and found they were not at home, he left a cowslip or an ivy leaf in the latch as his personal calling card.

At one time the cowslip was known as Herb Peter. A German legend tells us that St Peter, who holds the keys to the Kingdom of Heaven, heard that some people were trying to enter by the back door instead of the front gates. This lack of reverence upset him so much that the keys fell from his hand, rooted in the earth below and grew into cowslips. Their German name is Himmelschlüsselchen, the little keys of heaven, and they are also known as Our Lady's key or the marriage key.

The sentiment associated with cowslips is pensiveness. It's a thought which we might take to heart if we are ever tempted to pick any of the rapidly-disappearing wild flowers which are part of our countryside heritage.

TUESDAY—JUNE 25.

SOME weeks after her grandfather died, five-year-old Samantha was rummaging through the dressing-table drawer.

"Mummy," she cried, "Grandad's gone to heaven without his glasses, and he won't be able to see a thing!"

SUMMER DREAM

THE FRIENDSHIP BOOK

I ONCE came home from work grumbling — everything and everybody seemed wrong. Some folk were working too slowly, others too quickly and not conscientiously enough, and the filing system was in a glorious muddle!

After I had got it all off my chest, the Lady of the House wasn't the least bit sympathetic. She told me tactfully that she had been reading a book by Aldous Huxley, and quoted to me what he said. It truly put me in my place, and it made me think.

He said: "There's only one corner of the universe you can be certain of improving and that's your own self."

Do you know, nothing seemed quite so bad at work ever again — or anywhere else after that, I have to say!

PSALM OF LIGHT

THE Lord is my lantern, I shall not falter,
He goes before me on the dark and lonely footpaths,
He lifts the shadows that wait around my door,
He lights the empty corners of my room,
In the greyness of doubt and uncertainty,
He will guide me.
In the darkness of hurt and despair,
I shall seek His brightness,
His light is constant and His comfort everlasting.
I shall travel with Him always,
And He will lead me safely on the journey of my life.
                                             Iris Hesselden.

FRIDAY—JUNE 28.

SOME years ago I recall helping out at a church jumble sale and, because it was hot work, I removed my jacket and put it to one side. Yes, you've guessed — it was accidentally sold by another helper!

With a little embarrassment, and good luck, I was able to buy it back again — and I still have it to this day! At the same time, a friendship was made with the purchaser which has also survived this length of time.

Isn't it often true that when something unexpected and a little inconvenient happens, we are shown a positive side to it all? I regained my coat — *and* found a new friend at the same time.

SATURDAY—JUNE 29.

I THINK that today there is more kindness around than we give people credit for. You have only to think of the care groups springing up all over the country to help folk — particularly the old and the infirm — with small jobs they are unable to do themselves.

Many of these groups' volunteers are retired or other not-so-young folk themselves. Nonetheless, they are most helpful, kind and generous with both their time and their money.

Anyone who is privileged to work with these circles knows how very grateful their clients are, and indeed what personal satisfaction such work brings.

SUNDAY—JUNE 30.

LET your speech be alway with grace, seasoned with salt, that ye may know how ye ought to answer every man.

Colossians 4:6

JULY

MONDAY—JULY 1.

"HALF the year gone already!" exclaimed the Lady of the House as she turned the calendar. We both paused for a moment to think about this.

The older we get, the faster time seems to fly. Do you remember how long we used to wait for our childhood birthdays? Then how the weeks dragged until our Summer holidays when we were young. As for Christmas — well, Christmas was an unbelievably long time in coming round each year.

"Never mind," I said, "we may have had half the year, but there's another half untouched and ready to start. Let's make the most of it!"

TUESDAY—JULY 2.

WE were helping to clear out a drawer that had not been tidied for years, and we came on a few unexpected treasures.

Among all the bric-a-brac there was a pamphlet issued by the government on "How To Keep Well In Wartime". As I read through it I found some sound advice — advice that, surprisingly, is still appropriate today.

There was a paragraph headed "What Makes You Worry?" which told how doctors constantly see the destructive effects of envy, jealousy and hatred. It said, "You will agree that the person who is kindly and tolerant is happier than the one who is not. Seeking happiness, you will strive to be kindly and tolerant, so watch for the first signs of hate and envy in yourself and nip them in the bud. Talk it over with someone."

I like that last sentence best of all.

THE FRIENDSHIP BOOK

WEEDS were creeping into our lawn and I was afraid that these unwanted intruders would take over, if not checked in some way. That's why I asked a gardening friend to recommend a good weedkiller.

Arthur named a few and then added, "I suggest you stop worrying about killing the weeds. Instead feed the grass — it will then grow faster and stronger and choke out the enemy."

I began right away by spraying extra goodness over my lawn. It worked and I rejoiced in the stronger growth of grass and the gradual disappearance of the invaders. I couldn't help thinking that maybe some other evils around me could be overcome, with just a little extra goodness on my part — and in so doing could maybe even help others to grow in strength.

"Be not overcome by evil, but overcome evil with good."   Romans 12:21.

THE Lady of the House met our District Midwife recently — that good lady has been practising for over 30 years, bringing thousands of new arrivals into the world.

She said, "I often think if I could wave a magic wand and give them a gift for life, what would it be? There is so much to choose from — beauty, brains, wealth, long life, a good-looking partner or outstanding talents, perhaps.

"However, I think I would choose a happy, serene childhood — for that brings contentment and an understanding heart in later life, and will stand a person in good stead right to the end. Can anyone think of a more desirable gift?"

Wise words indeed.

THE FRIENDSHIP BOOK

S UPPOSE *we were put up for auction,*
  How much do you think we'd be worth?
  Our value would vary with all sorts of facts:
  Our virtues, our failings, intentions and acts,
From today to the hour of our birth.

And features we used to be proud of
Might fetch just a humble amount.
  But helpful words uttered a long time ago,
  And deeds, long forgotten, new richness could show
With surprising reward, beyond count!

So who can assess what our worth is?
How we stand in the other man's eyes?
  The young judge the old, and age judges youth:
  Perhaps it's as well that we don't know the truth,
It could be a shock . . . and surprise!
                                        Noel Scott.

IT was good to hear about John Horton who was included in the 1992 Queen's Birthday Honours for his work as a road sweeper.

He had overcome a mental handicap, and for 30 years until his retirement, had devoted his life to keeping the roads of East Staffordshire clean and tidy. John was recommended for the British Empire Medal by the County Council, and it was presented to him by the Lord Lieutenant of Staffordshire. It was said of him: "His commitment to the job is above reproach. He is an example to us all in encouraging a cleaner environment."

So I am proud to raise my hat to John, and to all those who have risen above adverse circumstances — and come out on top!

H

THE FRIENDSHIP BOOK

THEN spake Jesus again unto them, saying, I am the light of the world: he that followeth me shall not walk in darkness, but shall have the light of life.

John 8:12

" I FEEL as if I'm surrounded by a thick hedge and just can't see my way through it," a friend said to me one day. Troubles can indeed seem like that.

John Wesley, the great preacher, was walking along a country lane with a man who was experiencing similar feelings to my friend: he'd reached the stage when he simply did not know what to do.

As they talked, John Wesley asked, "Do you know why that cow is looking over the hedge?" The question sounded foolish to the troubled man, and he shook his head.

"That cow is looking *over* the hedge because she cannot see through it, and this is what you must do with your troubles — look above, and over them," came the reply.

It *does* work — you get a completely new perspective on the view ahead.

SOMETIMES the fewest words have the greatest impact, which is perhaps why those old autograph albums contained such memorable gems. Here is a Chinese proverb which might be of encouragement to you today:

Tell me — I forget
Show me — I remember
Involve me — I understand.

THE FRIENDSHIP BOOK

I ONCE injured my ankle, and it took several weeks to heal properly. I love walking, so until I had come to terms with the situation I felt very frustrated.

The first thing I did when I could get out again was to go into the countryside. It was Summer and there was a heady perfume in the lane. The hedgerows were full of clumps of colourful, scented flowers. Nobody had cut the verges or used pesticides and here they were — pink, yellow, and purple, a blaze of colour blooming to perfection.

I lingered for a while, standing firmly on both feet, and was so thankful for being able to get out and about to enjoy the beauty around me.

Because of a weak ankle I found that I had learned a valuable lesson — how to make the best of the worst, and the most of the best.

THANK YOU FOR TODAY

THANK You for this day, Lord,
And for the wind and rain,
We think of many barren lands
Where no-one would complain.
Thank You for the time we shared
And for our plans and schemes,
We think of people round the world
Who lost their hopes and dreams.
Thank You for life's simple things,
For blessings on the way,
For all we take for granted, Lord,
And thank You for today.

Iris Hesselden.

THE FRIENDSHIP BOOK

A FRIEND told a nice story recently of how, when his grandparents were married many years ago, they started to call small wedding presents by the names of those who'd given them.

A small vase to hold violets was always known as Mrs Pearson, a little salt cellar was John Green (the coalman who delivered their first sack of coal), and Louise and Lottie Smith were the two pretty egg cups which they used most days.

Grandmother explained that this unusual christening was done so friends would not be forgotten in the rush and bustle of life. She knew she would remember the folk who gave large presents, but felt she might forget who sent smaller ones.

Her "little friends" were never forgotten, and she often used to speak of them. I think it is a lovely idea — an unusual one worth copying today!

"IT'S one of my lazy days today, Francis," said our friend Mary as we went into her sitting-room. "I didn't sleep too well so I'm taking things easily."

As I began to express my sympathy, Mary said, "Oh, don't worry about me. Lying awake doesn't trouble me at all. It gives me the opportunity to think about all those who *have* to stay awake during the night — the shift-workers, policemen, those at sea, hospital doctors and nurses and those who are kept awake by pain, and all the mothers who may be soothing fretful babies. As I think about them, I say a little prayer for each of them — and then I am able to lie contentedly in my own warm, comfortable bed."

I believe I have mentioned before that a visit to Mary usually gives me a lot to think about!

A WAY OF LIFE

THE FRIENDSHIP BOOK

VERILY I say unto you, Except ye be converted, and become as little children, ye shall not enter into the kingdom of heaven.

Matthew 18:3

MONDAY—JULY 15.

FOR as long as I can remember, Joan has had a hobby — writing. She combines writing poetry with her journalism, and recently she has started to write songs as well, in her spare time. She also puts them to music. This is a real challenge, and Joan likes nothing better. "Composing poems is not so difficult, but writing music to fit the words isn't all that easy," she remarks.

As a girl, Joan was compelled to take music lessons, learn all the theory, and sit the examinations, but later she just followed her own natural inclination towards words. Now, her present hobby combines both interests. I always tell her that she has a song in her heart — because she shares her gifts with others.

If we have a hobby which gives us pleasure and satisfaction, it is worthwhile; but if the same hobby gives a little of that pleasure to others, then it is a treasure house.

TUESDAY—JULY 16.

IN the parish church hall at Wormit in Fife I spotted a notice with a difference. In place of the usual admonition to turn off heaters, a sign reads: "If you have turned off the heaters, please turn them on again before you leave for the benefit of the next people to come in."

That's true Christian warmth.

THE FRIENDSHIP BOOK

"AN old dodderer". When we hear this description we see it as one of derision, usually applied by someone young and disrespectful. Bramwell Evans, remembered with affection by many of an older generation as "Romany" of radio fame, had a different idea in mind when he told a war-time audience:

"When you get fed up with present-day happenings, go out into the lanes and the fields, and listen and look at the things of nature. There is no hurry in that world — that is why I am a dodderer. I lose all sense of time when I'm in the country, and forget the speed of machinery. To be a dodderer is a lost art these days, one that we should recapture."

I like to think that I, too, can be a dodderer sometimes.

WHEN Connie, who is disabled, decided to ask a painter, Mr McDonald, to do the outside of her bungalow, she didn't realise how much it would be to the benefit of both of them.

She was so pleased with his work and pleasant manner that she recommended him to her friends and neighbours, and it wasn't long before his van was to be seen outside other houses in the avenue. The work snowballed and for the whole of the Summer he was kept fully employed — just because of one person's recommendation.

For his part, Mr McDonald was very good to Connie. He did little bits of shopping for her and was willing to replace light bulbs and attend to any small things around the house that she was unable to do for herself.

Truly, one good turn deserves another!

MOST great actors and performers prefer a live audience. Why should this be so? The famous Russian violinist David Oistrakh provides an answer. After giving a concert in an auditorium with many musical experts present, he was asked how he enjoyed playing to such a critical assembly.

"It was wonderful," he said, "they created an atmosphere of attentive intimacy. It was as if all were helping to turn the pages of my music."

Is it not the same in everyday life? We experience such an uplift of spirit when those around us show appreciation and cooperation, and because of this we are thereafter more inclined to praise rather than censure, to be helpful rather than obstructive. We feel inspired — as if all about us are helping to turn the pages of life.

COMFORT

THE right kind of words in sorrow
  Are often so hard to say,
But a gentle tone, and a clasping hand
  Can ease the distress away.
For just being there, will mean so much
  When someone feels alone,
And the comfort spread in the strength you give
  Brings a warmth in the kindness shown.

Elizabeth Gozney.

O LORD our Lord, how excellent is thy name in all the earth!

Psalms 8:9

THE FRIENDSHIP BOOK

IF, like me, you thought that the use of dogs in guiding blind people was an idea that originated in the 20th century, then you will be very surprised to learn that it is a much older custom. When the ruins of Pompeii were excavated after lying buried under the volcanic ash from Mount Vesuvius, they revealed wall paintings of a blind man being led by his dog. Remember — Pompeii was buried in 79 AD.

The first training schools were established in Germany just before the First World War, and dogs were used on battlefields to track down the wounded and to lead blinded soldiers to safety. However, it was not until 1931 that the British Guide Dog Association was founded and four German Shepherd dogs were trained by the National Institute for the Blind.

Now there are seven training centres in Leamington, Exeter, Bolton, Forfar, Wokingham, Middlesbrough and Redbridge, and 4000 working guide dogs. The most suitable breeds for training are German Shepherds, Labradors and Golden Retrievers. During the four-month training period, the dogs learn the discipline of keeping their sightless owner safe in every situation in the home or outdoors.

Humans have the greatest affection for their own particular pet, but the relationship between blind people and their guide dogs is even more special because it depends entirely on the complete trust which is so essential between the guided and the guiders.

A FRIEND is a person with whom I may be sincere. Before him I may think aloud.

Ralph Waldo Emerson.

THE FRIENDSHIP BOOK

JUST take a walk through a park, and I'll guarantee you'll see or hear something to make you think! I always do . . . one windy afternoon I saw an elderly lady and a small boy flying kites.

"Pull harder, Gran!" yelled the boy. They both pulled, and together they laughed as the two kites soared and dipped together. I stopped and joined in the moments of shared happiness. Then an ice-cream van came along, and the kites were pulled in while Gran bought two cones.

"My goodness, isn't this fun!" she laughed. "Now if my daughter was here, she'd say, 'Mum, be your age!' Why should I, at *my* age? Homes are full of old ladies 'being their age'!"

You'll never be one of them, I thought — not while you still have such a zestful outlook on life.

CHILDREN have their own individual ways of interpreting stories they hear at Sunday school. I have to thank a church magazine for the following story about a ten-year-old boy recounting a lesson.

"Our teacher told us how God sent Moses behind the enemy lines to rescue the Israelites from the Egyptians. He brought them to the Red Sea and ordered his engineers to build a pontoon bridge. After they had all crossed, Moses looked up and saw the Egyptian tanks coming. He grabbed his walkie-talkie and ordered his airforce to bomb the bridge and save the Israelites."

His mother looked doubtful. "Are you sure, David, that is how your teacher told the story?"

"Well, not exactly, but if I told you what she said, you'd never believe it!"

FRIDAY—JULY 26.

OUR friends Tom and Vera were having a good laugh when the Lady of the House and I called to see them recently. They were having to apply for new passports before taking a holiday abroad, and had just collected the small head and shoulders photographs from the studio.

Passport pictures are rarely flattering, and these were no exception. "Mine makes me look like a convict!" declared Tom, laughing. I assured him he was exaggerating, but I was reminded of a story about Pope John XXIII.

While sitting for an official photograph, His Holiness sighed, "God knew 77 years ago that one day I'd be Pope. Why couldn't He have made me more photogenic?"

His multitude of followers no doubt preferred him as he was.

SATURDAY—JULY 27.

HOW I agree with Victor Hugo:
"My coat and I live comfortably together. It has assumed all my wrinkles, does not hurt me anywhere, has moulded itself on my deformities, and is complacent to all my movements, and I feel its presence only because it keeps me warm. Old coats and old friends are the same thing."

SUNDAY—JULY 28.

GIVE unto the Lord, ye kindreds of the people, give unto the Lord glory and strength. Give unto the Lord the glory due unto his name; bring an offering, and come before him; worship the Lord in the beauty of holiness.

Chronicles I 16:28-29

ROSES ARE RED,
SKIES ARE BLUE...

A N old proverb says: "You may light another's candle from your own without loss."

How true it was, and still is: a person could light their candle from the flame of your candle, yet your own flame did not burn any less brightly. So it is with happiness, joy, and good news — we can share them with others, without losing any intensity of feeling whatsoever. In fact, because we've *shared* the light, it now beams more brightly than ever.

EVERY DAY

A RE you casting about for life's purpose?
Are you drifting in aimless despair?
Reach out, put your trust in the Saviour,
And start every day with a prayer.

All the pressures of life that surround you,
The temptations you meet everywhere,
They will never be able to ground you
If you start every day with a prayer.

Alice Christianson.

T HE other day I came across an encouraging equation devised by a lady named Janet Colman, which made use of all the traditional aspects of arithmetic.

She advised: "To work out our life problems, we need to add love; subtract hate; multiply good; and divide between truth and error."

Worth thinking about, isn't it?

AUGUST

THURSDAY—AUGUST 1.

AROMATHERAPY has become quite popular nowadays — and not only with the ladies.

It is a system of massage using essential oils from many plants and flowers, in order to release the body from tension. The oils may be obtained from plants such as roses or evening primroses, although lavender is the one most frequently used for promoting relaxation. The effects are said to be very beneficial.

Yet a course of aromatherapy is a real luxury, for the smallest phial of an essential oil does not come cheaply. On the other hand, we may wander through a meadow of sweet-smelling flowers on a Summer's afternoon, or soak up the wonderful scent of honeysuckle at dusk.

To my mind, nothing could be more restful, and what's more it is entirely free — God's own gift of aromatherapy!

FRIDAY—AUGUST 2.

IT was a sad day when the children's pet hamster died. Eight-year-old Hannah decided that a formal funeral was called for, so she obtained a small box, and a little hole was dug at the bottom of the back garden.

Eventually Hannah, with her five-year-old brother Thomas by her side, stood there with hands clasped and eyes closed, giving thanks for all the joy and fun their late pet had brought them. They ended with a fervent "Amen."

Then five-year-old Thomas added, "Oh, Jesus, do be careful and put your gloves on before you pick her up — because she bites!"

THE FRIENDSHIP BOOK

HARRY MILLER of Worthing sent me this thoughtful poem entitled "Cock-Sure" which gives us much to think about:

> *Yes, I'm a Christian — of course I am.*
> *Well, sort of, that is, not a church man.*
> *No time to waste on hullabaloo —*
> *Somewhere distant a cock crew.*
>
> *What's mine is mine and none to spare,*
> *I will not give and will not share.*
> *No time to spend on the needy few —*
> *A second time the cock crew.*
>
> *Won't bend my knee to anyone,*
> *Belief in God all dead and gone.*
> *To see and touch for me is true —*
> *Thrice distant now, the cock crew.*

FOR whoso findeth me findeth life, and shall obtain favour of the Lord.

Proverbs 8:35

OUR friend Julia was very disappointed when her husband forgot her birthday, and she accused him tearfully of not caring about her any more.

Her husband smiled and said, "Darling, how am I supposed to remember your birthday when you never seem to look any older?"

As Julia remarked later, how could she possibly remain angry after that?

THE FRIENDSHIP BOOK

ONE hot Summer afternoon I sat on the rocks beneath an azure sky, watching the incoming tide. As the waves rolled farther and farther along the shore, they surged between the inlets, lapping round the rocks and loosening scraps of litter left behind by holidaymakers. Eventually the tide turned, taking all it had reclaimed and leaving behind the sand, smooth and clean once more.

Just like life, I thought. We may have made mistakes during the day and been aware of our shortcomings and failures, yet each night we have the opportunity to reflect and to put our house in order.

Once we have swept away all the debris, we know we can meet the next day with a perfectly clean sheet. That's something I find very reassuring!

WEDNESDAY—AUGUST 7.

ONE of the most famous and remarkable books of this century is "The Seven Pillars of Wisdom" by T. E. Lawrence, the man often referred to as Lawrence of Arabia. In the book he tells of his work and friendship with the Arabs, and of how he tried to do his best for his own country.

Lawrence had just finished writing his book when he took the manuscript with him on a journey to check it over before sending it to the publisher. As he got out of the train, he gathered up his belongings, but left behind the manuscript that he had worked on for so long. He never saw it again.

That might have been the end of the story, but it wasn't. He sat down and wrote his book all over again — the book that we still read today.

It is a splendid example of how determination can sweep aside all obstacles.

THE FRIENDSHIP BOOK

ONE of the pleasantest ways I know of spending a Summer afternoon, is to explore an old churchyard. You learn a little history, enjoy a small portion of philosophy, reflect on Nature, all amidst perfect peace and serenity.

Once, the Lady of the House and I visited an ancient village church, cool and shadowy inside, surrounded outside by bright, wild flowers. Butterflies hovered and birds sang — it was impossible to feel sad. We sat for a while on an oak bench, basking in the beauty.

Later, wandering between the weathered headstones, we studied the inscriptions. Many were half obliterated by years of rain and frost, but others were easier to decipher. One, which brought a smile to our faces, said simply: "Poet, Philosopher, Failure"! We felt we would have liked this person, a humble soul, but not without a sense of humour.

Another one appealed greatly to us:

The wonder of the world,
The beauty and the power,
The shapes of things,
Their colours, lights and shades,
These I saw.
Look ye also while life lasts.

Isn't it true that the wonders of the world are all around us, if we only take time to stop and look?

"WHEN one door of happiness closes, another opens; but often we look so long at the closed door that we do not see the one which has been opened for us."

Helen Keller.

THE FRIENDSHIP BOOK

MANY CHAPTERS

THEY say that life is like a book
So what kind can it be?
A history? A mystery?
We'll have to wait and see;
The plot has many twists and turns,
A most enthralling text,
I find it so exciting
To wonder what comes next!

D.J. Morris.

GIVE unto the Lord, O ye mighty, give unto the Lord glory and strength.

Psalms 29:1

MANY people have a favourite hymn, and one of mine begins: "Dear Lord and father of mankind, forgive our foolish ways."

Why this one in particular? Well, I suppose it's because of the reminder it gives of the unhappiness we can sometimes cause without ever intending to do so. It is rarely on purpose that we put off fulfilling promises, or lending a hand to those in need; and it is rarely deliberate malice that causes us to pass on that interesting tit-bit of gossip about a friend or neighbour. Nevertheless, the heartache which results may be considerable.

Next time we feel tempted to "tut-tut" over the folly of others, perhaps it might be just as well to spare a thought for our own "foolish ways".

THE FRIENDSHIP BOOK

ANN had been to a coffee morning to raise funds for one of the well-known animal charities.

There was a tombola stall and she had bought tickets, but since she isn't usually lucky she didn't expect to win a prize. However, to her amazement she had indeed picked a winning ticket, and won a pack of tiny reels of coloured thread.

It was such a useful idea to have a small quantity of so many different colours. So often a button comes off a garment or a hem starts to fall down, and there isn't any thread of the right colour in the house.

In our daily lives, too, we need a small amount of colour to brighten our days and help to combat our worries and disappointments. Who hasn't felt an uplift of spirits on seeing a patch of blue sky, or a glowing display of Summer flowers?

On a gloomy day let us all look for our own patches of colour.

IN one of our church newsletters recently I came across this anonymous little poem appropriately entitled "Not Bad":—

> *I've never met a perfect saint —*
> *We all slip up a lot.*
> *I've never met a villain who*
> *Had not one kindly thought.*
> *So I am slow to pick upon*
> *The faults I find in others,*
> *And try to see what good there is*
> *In all my erring brothers!*

I quite agree — don't you?

THE FRIENDSHIP BOOK

WHEN a friend retired he tried to describe the experience to me. "The difference between working life and retirement," he said, "is like shopping for the necessities of life and window shopping!"

He went on, "When we are shopping for necessities we usually have to do this in a hurry. We perhaps enjoy it, but not completely.

"Now, window shopping," he said with satisfaction, "is like retirement. We can look around and savour the moment. Unlike window shopping, though, what you see has nothing to do with possessions. It is what I'd call real wealth, but yields no financial dividends."

I liked his comparison. At 85 Jim is still strolling along the lanes near his home, and still exclaims with delight how much he is excited by the riches of the changing seasons. He is still enjoying his "window shopping"!

ANOTHER friend, John, was taken into hospital for an operation about which he was very worried.

However, before getting into bed that first evening, he had a brief chat with other patients on the ward. One of them, Ronald, had been bedridden for two years with a spinal problem. What amazed John was Ronald's forward-looking outlook.

"Two years I've been like this," he said, "and in another nine months I might be able to sit up again. Won't that be wonderful?"

Acknowledging that patience hadn't so far been his strongest point, John thoughtfully got into his bed and gave thanks for Ronald's remarkable endurance, then asked that he, too, might be given such courage.

AT REST

SATURDAY—AUGUST 17.

K EEP faith and hope within your heart,
Though trials come your way;
We all must face them sometime —
It could be now, today.
Just do your best and carry on,
For what will be, will be,
And with the Lord to help you,
You'll stay the course — you'll see.

SUNDAY—AUGUST 18.

N OW unto the King eternal, immortal, invisible, the only wise God, be honour and glory for ever and ever. Amen.

Timothy I 1:16-17

MONDAY—AUGUST 19.

H ERE are a few more points to ponder from my collection of quotations:

A kitchen should be clean enough to be healthy
And dirty enough to be happy!

A good wife and health are a man's best wealth.

Words are like medicine; they should be measured with care, for an overdose may hurt.

If the stars appeared only once every ten years, everyone would rush out to see them.

He who is resting upon his laurels may be wearing them in the wrong place.

Diplomacy gets you out of what tact would never have allowed you to get into in the first place.

THE FRIENDSHIP BOOK

MANY folk, I feel sure, make a little bit extra when jam-time comes round, so that they may give a pot or two to others who are not able to make it for themselves.

The Lady of the House and I once made a trip to pick raspberries and strawberries, which after a week of sunshine were at the peak of perfection. As we waited to pay, the Lady of the House fell into conversation with someone who had filled several containers.

"It looks as if you are going to be busy making jam."

"Well, no," came the reply. "You see, these are all for an old people's nursing home. My mother was looked after there for many years, until just a few weeks before her 100th birthday. During that time I became friendly with the staff who'd cared for her so well, and each year I make sure that the residents and staff have a strawberry tea."

What a lovely way of making sure that these old folk have a share in the fruits of Summer — and it is just as nice when someone who has cause to be grateful returns to say "thank you".

OUR young friend, George, aged 13, got up late one Sunday morning — and I've a feeling this was more by design than by accident.

Coming downstairs he apologised, saying, "I'm afraid I'm too late to go to church this morning."

His father retorted, "No, George, you're just in time to go to church, but I'm afraid you are too late to have any breakfast!"

BRIDGE OF
SMILES

THE FRIENDSHIP BOOK

MIRACLES really do happen. Dr Sangster, the well-known Methodist minister, told a large wartime congregation in Westminster Central Hall, London, of one that happened to a friend of his. Dr Sangster was involved, too.

It seems that he was "visiting" in the West End after an air raid. "Suddenly," he told his enthralled listeners, "I heard a voice from within telling me to go to the East End. I disobeyed it and continued on my way — but the voice persisted, so I made my way to the East End. 'Where now?' I thought, not knowing where the little voice inside was directing me!

"I went down several streets and it then stopped at a certain house. I knocked and a woman answered, beaming with delight. I was invited in, then she reminded me that I had buried her husband a year ago. That morning in her loneliness she had prayed, 'Please send Dr Sangster to me today' — and there I was!"

The widow was at that service and later met people who became lifelong friends. If all that isn't a miracle, what is?

IT'S no good feeling bitter
It's no good feeling sad
It's no good always longing
For the things we've never had.
Far better to be hopeful
And face life with a grin,
Open up your heart and mind
And let the goodness in.

                    D.J. Morris.

SATURDAY—AUGUST 24.

FIFTY years ago Europe had been left scarred by the Second World War. It was at that time when it was resolved to hold an annual Eisteddfod in the beautiful Vale of Llangollen. Surely it would help to return the world to normality.

When the first German choir appeared on the platform, there was apprehension as to how they would be received. The Welsh presenter was uncertain about how to introduce them, for he had lost loved ones during the war. Then, in a burst of inspiration, he said, "Let us welcome OUR FRIENDS from Germany." There was a great burst of applause from the audience and the members of the choir were not the only ones with tears in their eyes.

Truly, as the logo on the Eisteddfod sweatshirts proclaimed some years later:

"Blessed is a world that sings. Gentle are its songs."

SUNDAY—AUGUST 25.

AND they were beyond measure astonished, saying, He hath done all things well; he maketh both the deaf to hear, and the dumb to speak.

Mark 7:37

MONDAY—AUGUST 26.

MY sister-in-law was very upset when she failed her driving test for the fourth time, but the examiner told her, "Don't think of the failure. Just think how much money you have saved on that celebration you were planning!"

Yes, I suppose that however disappointed we are at times, there is nearly always a bright side if only we look for it.

THE FRIENDSHIP BOOK

THE other day a Quaker acquaintance told me this story about the preacher Charles Haddon Spurgeon.

He was staying with a Quaker friend and told her that he had never been to one of their Meetings. When Sunday came round she took him to the Meeting House. He had heard about the quietness of the services, but when he actually experienced the silence — nobody saying a word — the great preacher could not contain himself. Perhaps they were all waiting for *him* to speak? Three times he whispered to his friend asking if he should rise, and three times she whispered to him, "No." At the end of the meeting she said to him, "Now you may speak."

That day the great preacher learned for himself that some gain as much strength and wisdom from silence as others do from speech and songs.

I HEARD of a friend who came home from work one day, exhausted and not in the best of tempers. His wife didn't quite know what to say to him.

Working under pressure, he had somehow accidentally broken the computer, which could not be repaired for some time. Our friend suffered all day from muttered complaints about his carelessness. He is a very quiet and calm person, always ready to help others, so afterwards, feeling very ashamed, his colleagues all sincerely apologised to him.

The Lady of the House summed up the situation by saying, "Surely he's learned by now that mistakes always attract more attention than virtues!"

She is right. We should, whatever the circumstances, always look for the virtues in others — not their mistakes.

GONE FISHING

THE FRIENDSHIP BOOK

WE all know that for years now, people have been trying to forecast exactly what the weather will be like, but have you ever noticed how sometimes the weather can forecast exactly what *people* are like?

For example, if on a gloomy, cloudy day you should chance to meet Mary Gold, she will smile, and tell you that the sun will soon break through. Meet Jimmy Grey, however, and he will shake his head grimly, assuring you that the rain will start any minute.

Likewise, on a glorious hot Summer's day, while Mary is busy inviting friends to tea in her garden, Jimmy will be muttering darkly of droughts and sunstroke.

Perhaps we all ought to be a little more careful next time we talk about the weather — we may be giving others a forecast of ourselves!

HAVE you ever come across this Chinese proverb? "Patience is power; with time and patience the mulberry leaf becomes silk."

How often this is proved true in life.

THE Lady of the House is usually in the garden at this time of year debudding the chrysanthemums. It is a job she thoroughly dislikes.

"It seems such a pity," she says, "to pick off all those little buds." Nevertheless, she knows it is essential if she is to have good strong plants with healthy blooms later on.

Isn't that just like life? We must eliminate our weaknesses while they are still buds, if our characters are to develop along the right lines.

SEPTEMBER

OBSERVE and hear all these words which I command thee, that it may go well with thee, and with thy children after thee for ever, when thou doest that which is good and right in the sight of the Lord thy God.

Deuteronomy 12:28

THE Lady of the House and I once stayed at a quiet guest house in the Cotswolds. The wheat was being harvested at the time, and by day our room looked out for miles on to the golden scene. Any sound that we heard in the night was the bleating of a faraway sheep, or a hedgehog snuffling under our window.

On the wall was a beautifully-worked piece of Victorian embroidery, and its simple message still stays in our mind when we think of that peaceful house and the view from the window:

Sleep sweetly in this quiet room
O thou — whoe'er thou art —
And let no mournful yesterdays
Disturb thy peaceful heart;
Nor let tomorrow mar thy rest
With dreams of coming ill.
The Maker is thy Changeless Friend;
His love surrounds thee still.
Forget thyself and all the world,
Put out each garish light.
The stars are shining overhead —
Sleep sweetly then. Goodnight.

SAND, SEA
AND SUMMER

THE FRIENDSHIP BOOK

I HAVE a dear friend, Martha, now in her late eighties, and like most elderly people, her memories are really important to her. One day she explained how she stores them.

"Do you know, Francis," she began, "I think my mind is full of tiny pigeon holes. Most of the time, I don't know just what they contain, but, now and then, I get a lovely surprise!"

She went on to tell how a name, a sound, or perhaps a certain scent, could unlock one of these pigeon holes, releasing reminiscences. Sometimes, something unexpected could transport her to another time and another place.

Recently, I have begun to understand even better just what Martha means. What a wonderful thing is the human mind and what a marvellous store house of treasure we all possess!

I WAS watching the Lady of the House arranging some roses that she had brought in from the garden to make the house look cheerful. Before she finished, she put some on my study desk.

In the cool of the evening as I sat looking at them, and thinking about them, one rose had already shed its petals. "The lives of all flowers are short," I thought, "but they always give of their best to us. Bloom succeeds bloom, far excelling the carved flowers in cathedrals, and flowers so cleverly made from silk."

When you think about it, our lives are transient like flowers, so we really should try to give of our best all the time that we are here.

The rose that lives its little hour
Is prized above the sculptured flower.

THE FRIENDSHIP BOOK

OUR good friend, Hermione, brought us a large basket of apples from her garden. "They are fallers," she told us, "and I must warn you to be careful, as some of them look perfect on the outside but when you cut them open they are rotten to the core. However, some don't look so good — they have scabs and bruises — but when you cut them open, you find they are perfect inside."

I couldn't help but think, "How like people." Some seem to be too good to be true until you get to know them well, and then you find they have quite a few flaws in their characters; while others don't appeal to you on first acquaintance, but turn out to be very loyal friends!

IN September our minds turn to harvest festivals. Older people often reminisce about the good times they had in the fields helping to bring in the harvest, and those of us who see pictures and listen to stories of these times perhaps wish that we had been there.

Anglo-Saxons called September Gerstmonath, "barley month", when the grain was harvested. It was also Halegmonath, the holy month of offerings when pagans gave thanks for the harvest.

Harvest today is quite different with modern technology and combine harvesters, but we still gather, either at church or in school for our harvest festivals, giving thanks to God. We should also spare a thought for parts of the world where there is famine, unlike our part of the world where there is plenty.

All year round — not just in September — as we give thanks for what we have, we must never forget there are others elsewhere in need.

THE FRIENDSHIP BOOK

RETURNING from a holiday recently, a friend brought me one of those attractive little pictures with a message on it, now so popular in tourist gift shops. They're the modern version of the Victorian sampler or text picture, I suppose.

The message was:

That Troublesome Task —
Do it NOW!

And, do you know, it's the best advice I've had for a long time! It is propped up on a shelf at eye-level, reminding me over and over again to get on with the things I least like doing. Get them over with, stop thinking gloomily about them — just take prompt action now. Then I can enjoy doing the things I *like* doing.

Such a lot of grumbling and useless dithering can be saved.

SET a watch, O Lord, before my mouth; keep the door of my lips.

Psalms 141:3

WHEN I was younger my grandmother used to encourage me to collect proverbs, and she was a great one at quoting just the right example at the appropriate moment.

I came across one I'm sure she never heard and I added it to my collection recently. It's an old Russian saying which goes:

"Horses of hope run fast, but asses of experience amble thoughtfully along."

A pleasant thought as we get older!

PARADISE VALLEY

THE FRIENDSHIP BOOK

THE HAPPY HOME

Farewell, little house, and thank you
  For the welcome you gave us there.
For the comfort in joy and sorrow,
  The feeling you really did care.
Farewell, little house, and thank you
  For the memories rich in each heart,
Which will help in the final moments
  When the time has come to part.
Farewell, little house, and bless you,
  As you blessed our lives every day —
And please! Will you give the new owners
  A welcome, in just the same way?

Elizabeth Gozney.

FARMERS are reputed to be great grumblers. That this has always been so is illustrated by the story of a farmer in the days of horses and carts. He was particularly noted for his grumbling.

If someone complimented him on a fine crop of wheat he would respond, with a groan, that his potatoes had failed. Next year fine potatoes would be cancelled out by poor grain harvests. No single year was ever wholly successful. Then one year the unthinkable happened; every crop was perfect and bountiful. Surely there could be no complaint?

"Bumper crops all round," a friend complimented him.

"Aye," came the farmer's stubborn reply, "and it nearly killed the horses bringing all the stuff in!"

Talk about being hard to please!

THE FRIENDSHIP BOOK

HAVE you ever admired a musician, artist or poet and sighed, "If only I had a talent like that?"

The truth is that every one of us has a gift or talent, but we have to search for it and then work hard at developing it. Are you good at making friends, telling jokes, encouraging young folk, or making people feel at ease? Perhaps you have never thought about it, but these are all God-given talents or gifts. We can use them to help our family, our friends and colleagues, or even complete strangers.

Albert Bayly, who was a United Reformed Church minister and well-known hymn writer, wrote this verse:

Lord of all good, our gifts we bring to Thee,
Use them Thy purpose to fulfil,
Tokens of love and pledges they shall be
That our whole life is offered to thy will.

The greatest gift of all — but even the humblest is beautiful in God's eyes.

A YOUNGSTER was out one day with his grandmother who hadn't been very well.

They made rather slow progress. Every parked car had to be examined and discussed, every moving one identified, all buses and lorries remarked upon.

Grandma didn't know a great deal about vehicles — but she was learning fast. Eventually, as they were nearing home, they saw an ancient Mini that had obviously seen better days.

"Look, Grandma!" the little boy exclaimed. "That Mini's been ill, like you."

From that day on, Grandma looked at old cars in a more sympathetic light.

THE FRIENDSHIP BOOK

"WHAT a lovely Summer it has been, Francis," remarked the Lady of the House one Autumn afternoon as she cut some of our remaining roses to put in the crystal vase that shows them off to such perfection.

"All the same, in some ways I'm not too sorry to see that season pass," she continued. "It's high time I potted my hyacinth bulbs; there's my new evening class to think about; and I'll have time to start on some dressmaking and read some of those long books I've been planning to do for ages. Before I know where I am, it will be time to be thinking of home-made mincemeat."

"Steady on there," I laughed, "you're wishing your life away!"

Still, I could understand her logic. With a philosophy like that there can be no regrets — today has been enjoyed to the full and there is something to be looked forward to tomorrow.

THEN Jesus answering said unto them, Go your way, and tell John what things ye have seen and heard; how that the blind see, the lame walk, the lepers are cleansed, the deaf hear, the dead are raised, to the poor the gospel is preached.

Luke 7:22

HERE are some wise words to ponder over today:

Room for improvement is the largest room in the world.

THE FRIENDSHIP BOOK

NOT long ago, I went for a walk down the street, in spite of the fact that it was a wet, miserable sort of day. Nearly everyone I met was grumbling about the weather, and making the usual complaints about the "typical British summer". However, one man greeted me with a broad grin and said, "Hello, Francis — lovely growing weather, isn't it?"

That reminded me of the visiting preacher who was known for his optimism and his ability to find something to give thanks for. He arrived at a village chapel one Sunday when it was blowing a gale and raining heavily. The congregation began to wonder what he would find to be thankful about on such a wild morning.

He proved himself equal to the occasion, and in his opening prayer he said, "We thank You, O Lord, that every day is not as bad as this one."

A STRANGE phenomenon — almost a miracle — occurs regularly, I'm told, in the dentist's surgery.

A man who has suffered for days from toothache at last plucks up the courage to visit his dentist. He sits in the chair and, at that very moment, his toothache disappears.

A dentist's secretary told a good story about a patient who was habitually late. On one occasion he rang to confirm an appointment, then added, "I'm afraid I'll be fifteen minutes late. That won't be a problem, will it?"

"Of course not," replied the long-suffering lady. "It just means we won't have time to give you an anaesthetic." Remarkably, he arrived on time.

Another miracle at the dentist's!

LEAVES AND EAVES

THE FRIENDSHIP BOOK

THE Lady of the House could not be blamed if she has felt a little jealous. You see, another member of her sex has taken to waiting outside the garden gate for me. When I set out for a walk, *she* comes, too. She follows me wherever I go until I get back to the gate and then she goes off to her own home a few doors away.

As I say, the Lady of the House might well be more than a bit put out. You'll understand why she isn't when I tell you that the other lady in my life is, in fact, a little West Highland terrier. She has found a way of slipping under her own gate and coming along to ours.

I think the "affair" is to be nipped in the bud, though. I saw her master examining the foot of his gate very closely one morning. The Lady of the House will be relieved!

HARVEST OF THE SPIRIT

LET those love now who never loved before,
   Whilst those who always loved, love even more.
Let all who feel rejected, seek and find
New hope, new warmth and healing peace of mind.
Let those who think their faith has ebbed away
Stretch out their hands, to grasp a brighter day.
Let those who are imprisoned, far and wide,
Find freedom, where all men walk side by side.
Let those who have abundant blessings, give
To those in dark despair, the will to live.
Let all who love, now sow and reap and share
The harvest of the Spirit — everywhere.

                                        Iris Hesselden.

THE FRIENDSHIP BOOK

MR JONES has lived at No. 27 most of his life. Last year his wife died and then their great friends of many years, at No. 29 next door, moved away to be near their married daughter.

Into 29 came a young couple, the McKays, with two children. They are from a different part of the country and Mr Jones was very depressed. "I've got nothing in common with them," he grumbled. "I wish I had my old neighbours back."

Then Mrs McKay knocked on his door to ask his advice on the best shops. Mr McKay dropped in to enquire about sporting clubs and adult evening classes. One of the youngsters turned up on his doorstep. "Could you please help me with my school project?" he asked. "It's about local history."

Mr Jones is now a changed man. "What a lovely family they are!" he enthuses. "Mr McKay noticed that my leg is a bit stiff so he has offered to dig the garden next Spring. I'm very lucky — I couldn't have better neighbours!"

FOR the law was given by Moses, but grace and truth came by Jesus Christ. No man hath seen God at any time; the only begotten Son, which is in the bosom of the Father, he hath declared him.

John 1:17-18

HERE'S something to think about today: —
Worry is interest paid on trouble before it comes due.

THE FRIENDSHIP BOOK

WHEN a friend's sister-in-law went to live in a small village, she joined the Women's Fellowship at the local church. The secretary asked her if she had any special skills, such as playing the piano.

"No," Ivy replied, adding that she was not musical at all.

"Well, perhaps you could do some needlework. Embroider the hassocks or something like that?"

Ivy shook her head.

"Well, what about giving a talk?" the secretary persisted.

Again Ivy had to disappoint, but suddenly she had a great idea. "I'm quite good at clapping," she offered.

The secretary laughed but had the good sense to reply, "Well, that's splendid! We have a lot of folk who do things, but very few who appreciate them. We could do with a few good clappers."

WHEN our friend, Rose, started to train as a nurse her first theory lesson was to study a list of attributes needed to make a good nurse. These included patience, kindness, energy, humour, intelligence, integrity and a sincere love of the job.

She studied the list, thinking she could never aspire to such perfection, and nearly gave up all idea of such a career there and then. However, on further reflection she realised that if she had only the last of these characteristics — a sincere love of the job — all the others would fall into place of their own accord.

How true that is of life. If we really love what we are doing, we do it well — and overcome most difficulties along the way.

THE FRIENDSHIP BOOK

A SOCIOLOGIST was writing a book about the difficulties of growing up in a large family, so he interviewed the mother of 13 children. After several basic questions, he asked, "Do you think all children deserve the full, impartial love and attention of a mother?"

"Of course," said the mother.

"Which of your children do you love the most?" he asked next, expecting to catch her out in self-contradiction.

Her answer came at once. "The one who is ill, until he gets well — and the one who is away, until he gets home."

This made him think of the Shepherd who left the 99 sheep, to find the one that was lost.

THE Lady of the House and I were going on holiday with a friend whom we'd arranged to pick up at his house, but on the morning of departure, the car was proving impossible to start. So, very early, I rang our friend to say we would be delayed.

Imagine my dismay when I discovered that I had dialled the wrong number, and a complete stranger answered. I offered my apologies for waking him.

Later, I re-dialled, but then realised, to my disbelief, that the same thing had happened. Profusely apologising once again, I was about to ring off, when the man at the other end said, "Please don't apologise, I've seen a most beautiful sunrise this morning. If you hadn't wakened me, I would have missed it."

His words made my day. Pleasures often arrive and are doubled, like Thomas Middleton's, "by many a happy accident."

SATURDAY—SEPTEMBER 28.

OUR friend Mary came to see us recently and told us of her brother who was once apprenticed to an old jeweller, a bit of a character. Whenever a young couple came to buy an engagement ring, the old man would give them advice on how to live together happily until a ripe old age.

One day, after his usual homily, Mary's brother said, "That was a good performance, sir — and all for a 30-shilling ring."

"Ah, my lad," the old man said, "Life without love is like a garden without flowers."

How true that is. How lost we would be without flowers — and without love!

SUNDAY—SEPTEMBER 29.

BUT this I say, He which soweth sparingly shall reap also sparingly; and he which soweth bountifully shall reap also bountifully.

Corinthians II 9:6

MONDAY—SEPTEMBER 30.

ALL went well during the service one Sunday until four-year-old Tommy decided that he needed a drink of water. He said he knew where to go and could go alone.

Dad agreed and Tommy went off alone down the aisle. After a few minutes, thirst quenched, he returned and stared at a sea of faces. He could not see his dad. Undeterred, he shouted up to the pulpit in a very loud voice, "Hey, Mister, can you see my dad from there?"

Dad was the one who was not smiling. Everyone else was.

OCTOBER

IT was a brisk, breezy Autumn day. Leaves were chasing each other around the park and clouds raced across the sky.

I thought how sad it is that some people find this time of year depressing. A lady I once knew said she hated the leaves. Perhaps they made her garden untidy. Whatever the reason, it seemed a great pity that she did not enjoy the glorious colours and richness of this season.

As we grow older, the prospect of Winter approaching can be a little daunting, I know, yet there are always compensations — cosy evenings by the fire, music to listen to and good books to read.

Perhaps we can think of Autumn as a time of reflection and thanksgiving. Not only for the Summer past, but also for many previous ones. Then we can face the colder weather cheerfully and even look forward to the Spring with new hope.

PRAYER FOR PATIENCE

FATHER, hear the prayer I pray,
Give me patience every day.
Teach me how to seek and find,
Quiet hope and peace of mind.
Thoughtful in my words and deeds,
Understanding others' needs.
Father, let me always be
Patient, as You are with me.

Iris Hesselden.

THE FRIENDSHIP BOOK

IN October 1991, the Spanish golfer Seve Ballesteros won the World Match Play golf championship at Wentworth. In the final he was playing Nick Price of Zimbabwe, and involuntarily coughed at the precise moment when Price was striking his ball — which promptly flew into a bunker.

Ballesteros immediately asked permission for Price to play the stroke again. Unfortunately, the rules would not allow this to be done, so rather than appear to take advantage of Price's mistake, Seve Ballesteros insisted on sharing that particular hole half-and-half, even though it posed the possibility of his losing the match.

To my way of thinking, that surely marks out Seve Ballesteros as one of the world's true sportsmen.

I WONDER if you ever stop to read the thoughts on our Wayside Pulpits? It's something the Lady of the House and I make a point of doing, and here are the latest additions to our collection:

For the best picture of the Father, don't have your back to the Son.

The heart of prayer is prayer from the heart.

Fight truth decay — brush up on the Bible every day.

Bibles which are falling apart are usually read by people who aren't.

Lord, help me to remember that nothing is going to happen to me today that you and I can't handle.

K

THE FRIENDSHIP BOOK

WHEN I met old Mrs Bradshaw in the park she told me that she'd been advised to go to the doctor for a flu jab.

"You know, Mr Gay," she said, "I was absolutely terrified. I nearly didn't go, but the District Nurse said it was a wise precaution. So I went along trembling from head to foot, but I didn't feel a thing. The anticipation was much worse than the realisation."

Isn't that often so? The trouble we dread so often disappears when we face up to it.

I LIKE the story of a Sunday school where the superintendent wanted the children to understand what they were doing when they made their offering.

He therefore asked them to quote a verse of Scripture to suit, and felt he was doing quite well, when one little girl produced: "The Lord loveth a cheerful giver"; and another boy referred to the verse: "It is more blessed to give than to receive."

However, he was a bit taken aback when the bright lad of the bunch said with a knowing smile, "A fool and his money are soon parted!"

A friend of mine retold the story at a Methodist Circuit Rally and then, announcing that the offering would be received, invited the company "to play the fool as effectively as possible."

NOR height, nor depth, nor any other creature, shall be able to separate us from the love of God, which is in Christ Jesus our Lord.

Romans 8:39

L

THE FRIENDSHIP BOOK

"**H**OW beautiful they are, Francis," said the Lady of the House, "and how they improve with age."

We were taking a stroll through the woods on a crisp, sunny day and the objects of her admiration were the trees, arrayed in their glorious Autumn coats of red, yellow, brown and gold.

"I always think of them as one of the bonuses of the back end of the year," she said, "and that is why I never feel sad once Summer is over, for there is always a surprise in store just around the corner."

Her remarks made me reflect on the many things that improve with age — the rich fruit cake that needs many weeks to mature if it is to reach perfection in time for the wedding day; the sheen that has grown on a treasured piece of furniture because of years of loving polishing; the playful and sometimes tiresome puppy that grows into a lovely and trustworthy companion; the satisfaction of a couple who see their children develop into responsible citizens with families of their own; the serene expression and steady eyes of a face that has experienced its share of the knocks and hardships of life — and survived them.

Yes, there's a great deal for us to be thankful for as we get older. I'm sure we could each make our own list!

WEDNESDAY—OCTOBER 9.

I CAME across this piece of advice recently and would like to share it with you today:

When doing things for yourself be guided by
  your head,
When doing things for others be guided by
  your heart.

THE FRIENDSHIP BOOK

MINISTERS, like many other people in public life, often find it difficult to remember a name and it can turn out to be quite embarrassing. A minister I heard about, who didn't wish to upset anybody through his forgetfulness, solved the problem quite neatly.

If he met someone he couldn't remember, he would chat warmly for a minute or two and then confess that her name had slipped his mind. The lady would probably give her surname and then he would reply, "Oh, yes, I *know* you are Mrs Phillips, it's your Christian name I can't remember." He would then be supplied with the answer.

On the other hand, if he was given the Christian name he would say, "Oh, yes, I *know* you are Jean, but it's your married name I was after."

It was a tactic that never failed; and because the acquaintance was reassured that only part of a name was forgotten, and not the person behind it, hurt feelings were avoided.

Diplomacy and tact — where would we be without them!

PLINY the Younger, the Roman writer and administrator, who was born AD 62, wrote nine books of readable and charming letters. He had this to say to a dilatory correspondent:

"You say there is nothing to write about. Then write to me that there is nothing to write about."

Few of us have something momentous and exciting to write about, every time we pick up a pen to start a letter, but it is the keeping in touch that matters, don't you agree?

MY FEATHERED FRIENDS

THE FRIENDSHIP BOOK

THERE'S nothing at all wrong in being a dreamer, as long as you don't just let it stop there. Martin Luther King used to say, "I dream things that never were and say 'Why not?' "

BUT the wisdom that is from above is first pure, then peaceable, gentle, and easy to be intreated, full of mercy and good fruits, without partiality, and without hypocrisy.

James 3:17

IRIS HESSELDEN, the Morecambe poet, wrote this lovely prayer for bedtime:

Just for tonight — take all my cares,
And brush all pain and doubt away,
Please send a little healing, Lord,
To soothe the wounding of the day.
Give me contentment through the dark,
A quiet sleep, rest and repair.
Plant in my heart new strength and hope
To combat trouble or despair.
So when tomorrow wakes the sky,
And I arise to meet the day,
Help me to do the best I can,
And walk with You along the way.
But until then, wrap me in love,
And keep me safe, though shadows creep,
Just for tonight — shut out the world,
And grant, Oh Lord, the gift of sleep.

THE FRIENDSHIP BOOK

IT was a beautiful Autumn day, crisp and golden, and the Lady of the House and I decided to take another of our walks and enjoy the sunshine.

There had been strong winds for some days; the leaves, which had fallen quite suddenly, crunched and rustled beneath our feet. A mild breeze whispered and the sky was blue. We agreed that it was good to be alive on this kind of glorious day.

As we followed the quiet lane, we came to a parking area where people picnic or admire the view. It was deserted, except for the litter left behind. How could people be so careless, we asked ourselves? In no time, the Lady of the House produced two neatly-folded carrier bags from her handbag.

"There you are, Francis," she said triumphantly, handing one of them to me. Together we filled the bags with rubbish and carried them to the nearest bin. It was then that we noticed two beautiful pansies that were blooming beautifully amongst the man-made mess. Their stems were longer than usual, and they lifted their heads proudly and seemed to smile at the sun. We smiled, too, as we looked at their purple faces and admired their courage, flourishing in adversity.

As the air grew colder and dusk came that evening, we remembered those brave little flowers. How wonderful Mother Nature is! She continues to give delight, in spite of anything man may do. We are shown beauty in the most unexpected places.

"THERE is only one pretty child in the world, and every mother has it."

Chinese Proverb.

THE FRIENDSHIP BOOK

OUR friend Sally lives in the country. When we visited her she told us that she was toying with the idea of moving from her upstairs bedroom into her warmer downstairs one.

"Still, I do like going upstairs to bed," she said, "because I like to look out of the window last thing at night to see the sheep. My brother is a sheep farmer, and when it is lambing time I look out and wonder if he will have to be up all night with his flock. I say an extra prayer, and somehow it makes me feel closer to him."

Here is a prayer for animals and those who look after them which perhaps you might like to use today:

"O God, you have made all living things and you love them all. Grant that men may give to them the care which they deserve, as creatures whom your hands have made and for whom your heart cares."

(William Barclay)

I ENJOY reading church magazines which "Friendship Book" readers send me from time to time, and am often amazed at the quality of the writing. A good example is this "Poem For Life" I found in a magazine sent to me from Yorkshire.

> *Money will buy —*
> *A bed, but not sleep*
> *Books, but not brains*
> *Food, but not appetite*
> *Finery, but not beauty*
> *A house, but not a home*
> *Medicine, but not health*
> *Luxuries, but not culture*
> *Amusement, but not happiness*
> *A church, but not heaven.*

THE FRIENDSHIP BOOK

IN the museum at Delphi there is a statue of a Greek charioteer which is pointed out to tourists as a model of perfection. It is beautifully crafted in every detail — both the front section designed for public viewing, and the parts that would not normally be seen, because the Ancient Greeks believed that when something was made in honour of the gods only the best was good enough and it should be as perfect as was humanly possible.

It brought to mind something Lord Forte, owner of one of the largest hotel and catering organisations in the world, wrote in his autobiography: "Five thousand years ago what I am saying was right. In five thousand years what I am saying will still be right: cleanliness, honesty, decency, respect for other people, politeness, good manners, integrity — they will never be old-fashioned."

Wise words indeed!

JESUS answered and said unto them, Go and shew John again those things which ye do hear and see: The blind receive their sight, and the lame walk, the lepers are cleansed, and the deaf hear, the dead are raised up, and the poor have the gospel preached to them.

Matthew 11:4-5

THIS saying tells us how to become wiser each day. Think about it — and try it.

"When you are ready to admit that you were wrong yesterday, you will be much wiser today."

THE FRIENDSHIP BOOK

*O PERFECT Love, all human thought
transcending,*
Lowly we kneel in prayer before Thy throne,
That theirs may be the love which knows no ending
Whom Thou for evermore dost join in one.

This must surely be the most widely chosen of all wedding hymns, yet perhaps few brides know anything about the shy woman who wrote it, Dorothy Frances Gurney.

It was January 1883 and Katherine Gurney, the daughter of a London vicar, was to be married at Brathay in the Lake District in three weeks' time. She had chosen the tune of her wedding hymn, but somehow the words of it didn't fit the occasion.

"Well, if no-one will disturb me I will go into the library and see what I can do," her sister Dorothy offered. Within a quarter of an hour she had returned with the completed hymn.

The bride was delighted with it. For a year or two it was used only privately at weddings, then it was included in "Hymns Ancient And Modern" and when Queen Victoria's granddaughter chose it for her wedding to the tune "Sandringham", its popularity increased rapidly.

We have no known photograph of Dorothy Frances Gurney to show us what she looked like, but the lovely thoughts she expressed in that special wedding gift to her sister will endure.

" THERE is no failure except in no longer trying."

Elbert Hubbard.

THE FRIENDSHIP BOOK

A BOUQUET was delivered for the Lady of the House when she was out. However, it was all a mystery to me. The card said: "With love and thanks from Tim, Joan and Alice".

When the Lady of the House arrived home, she explained the mystery. On Saturday morning she had found a little girl, Alice, crying her eyes out in the street. After asking her name, the Lady of the House enquired, "What's the matter?"

"It's my birthday. I had a new dress and a bicycle this morning, and I'm going to have a party with a cake Mummy has made," was the sobbed reply.

"So why are you crying?"

"Because I'm lost!" wailed little Alice.

The Lady of the House soon found where Alice lived, and took her home to her anxious parents. So now they have found where we live, and another friendship has been forged — through a simple act of kindness.

E VANGELISM is the practice of spreading the Christian gospel, and the last ten years of the 20th century have been declared "The Decade of Evangelism". It was the vision of Father Tom Forrest, one of the Pope's private secretaries, who felt that God had planted in his heart a desire to see a world which was more Christian by the year 2000.

Taken up by almost every other major Christian Church throughout the world, the Decade commenced on 1st January 1991, its aim being to spread the gospel of peace and revitalise the Church in every land, by the efforts of you in your small corner and I in mine.

So let us see what contribution we can make today.

THE FRIENDSHIP BOOK

I'M not always certain what others mean when they talk about charity. Many would associate the word with giving help to the poor or less fortunate. In a general sense we are told that the word expresses the sentiment of love. I thought the explanation I read in a Baptist Church magazine recently made all the shades of meaning perfectly clear:

WHAT IS CHARITY?

It is silence, when words would hurt;
It is patience, when your neighbour is curt;
It is deafness, when scandal flows;
It is thoughtfulness for another's woes;
It is promptness, when duty calls;
It is courage, when misfortune falls.

Having read that I think I have a much clearer idea of what charity is all about.

IF ye then be risen with Christ, seek those things which are above, where Christ sitteth on the right hand of God. Set your affection on things above, not on things on the earth.

Colossians 3:1-2

I THINK that Euripides was right so long ago when he wrote:

"It is a good thing to be rich, and a good thing to be strong, but it is a better thing to be beloved of many friends."

TUESDAY—OCTOBER 29.

JUST for today I'll try to improve my soul in three ways:

I will do somebody a good turn, and not get found out;

I will do at least two things I don't want to do — just for exercise;

And today, if my feelings are hurt, I will not show it to anyone.

WEDNESDAY—OCTOBER 30.

SOMEONE once said that dreams are wisps of hope hidden in our souls.

The Lady of the House often daydreams. It is when life seems drab that she has her most vivid dreams, and I am privileged to share them.

"I can see us now, Francis, in a cottage with a sun-drenched thatch and a door facing the morning sun. We'll have two comfy old chairs and a cat to rub against our legs, and shelves full of our favourite books. You will keep bees, and I'll have a garden to tend with a hedge of lavender, a patch of herbs, and damask roses.

"We'll have our friends round to share our peaceful evenings — the knowledgeable ones who also have a sense of humour, and, when you are away, Francis, I'll always watch the clock with eager eyes, waiting for your return."

Could anyone wish for more?

THURSDAY—OCTOBER 31.

A HEATHEN philosopher once asked a religious man, "Where is your God?"

The man answered, "Let me first ask you, where is He not?"

NOVEMBER

FRIDAY—NOVEMBER 1.

I WAS once walking along Cheapside in London, and outside Bow Bells Church was a flower-seller. The flowers in front of me made a perfect picture on a dull November day.

As I passed the stall, an elderly lady paused to ask the price of the violets. They were evidently too expensive, for she walked on in front of me. Then something memorable happened.

A young man, who'd been behind the lady in the queue, had noticed what had happened. He bought some violets, caught up with the lady, tapped her on the shoulder, then very graciously presented her with the posy. Then he very quickly walked away, leaving her no time to thank him.

I later found that the same lady was sitting beside me on the Underground. Not knowing that I had seen the incident, she told me all about it. "It made me feel quite young again," she said, obviously thrilled.

It is these little acts of inspirational kindness that can make life so much brighter.

SATURDAY—NOVEMBER 2.

THIS advert, displayed in the window of a Christian bookshop, made me smile. Someone had taken two lines from a hymn:

Satan trembles when he sees
The weakest saint upon his knees.

and changed the couplet to:

Satan trembles when he sees
Christian books as cheap as these.

THE FRIENDSHIP BOOK

SUNDAY—NOVEMBER 3.

THEN said Jesus unto them, When ye have lifted up the Son of man, then shall ye know that I am he, and that I do nothing of myself; but as my Father hath taught me, I speak these things.

John 8:28

MONDAY—NOVEMBER 4.

ONE winter the boiler broke down, leaving the house without hot water or central heating during a really cold spell. There was also an electricity cut, so there was no light and I had to make do with candles and spent a miserable day until the faults were located and repaired.

It was then I started thinking of the old folk of yesteryear, who did not have the benefit of modern comforts. Perhaps we should all stop and count our blessings for the marvellous innovations that science has given us today.

TUESDAY—NOVEMBER 5.

BEHOLD, a row of shining supermarket trolleys all looking alike — but acting alike? Oh, no!

Each trolley has a mind of its own — it goes right when you want to go left; its wheels lock when you need to go ahead; and it likes nothing better than to charge a trolley more heavily laden than itself!

Frustrating? Aggravating? Yes — but next time you're confronted with such a self-willed monster, just think how good for your character it is to master these difficulties, rather than let its bad habits get the better of you.

The same can be said for life outside the supermarket.

THE FRIENDSHIP BOOK

HAVE you ever played Scrabble? It's one of the things the Lady of the House and I enjoy doing, particularly on a Winter's evening when we have drawn the curtains to shut out the chilly dark.

We are evenly matched, so we have some exciting games, but it always causes consternation if one of us picks up the letter Q towards the end of the game — and there is no U to go with it!

Scrabble players will know that Q is valued at 10 points, the highest scoring letter, whilst U rates only one point. Without U to accompany it, though, Q is nearly always quite useless — a liability, in fact.

This serves to remind me that whether we are a high-flying Q or a more modest U kind of person, we need one another. No man is an island and sometimes we need to be content to play a small and supportive role, in order that someone else can be free to play a more important part.

More often than not, in the end, we can bask in the reflected glory!

A COUNTRY minister took as the text for his sermon a line from St Matthew: "And Peter's wife's mother lay sick of a fever."

The following Sunday he continued on the same theme, and again the next week.

On Monday, two elderly members of the congregation were walking past the church when the bell began to toll.

"Who's that for?" asked one.

"I don't know," replied the other, "but I expect it's for Peter's wife's mother. She's been lying sick these past three weeks!"

CAMARADERIE

FRIDAY—NOVEMBER 8.

WHEN the Lady of the House and I called to see our old friend Mary, her eyes lit up.

"Oh, do come in!" she beamed. "You're just the people I want to see," and she led us into her tiny sitting-room.

"Look what I've got," she said, spreading out a lovely white linen tablecloth. "I'm asking all my friends to sign their name on it. Even little Joseph next door is going to be included, though he can hardly write yet! And then I'm going to have a lovely time these Winter afternoons embroidering all the signatures in every colour of the rainbow. It will be a lasting reminder of all the nice people I know, and as I work on each one, I'll think about that person. It will bring back such happy memories."

What a delightful idea! Mary's friends will be with her every time she spreads that lovely cloth on the table.

SATURDAY—NOVEMBER 9.

I WAS amused by the story about the little girl who asked if her grandmother could keep a secret.

"Oh, yes," replied Grandma.

"Well, you mustn't tell one to me," said the little girl, "because *I* can't."

SUNDAY—NOVEMBER 10.

THE Lord is gracious, and full of compassion; slow to anger, and of great mercy. The Lord is good to all: and his tender mercies are over all his works. All thy works shall praise thee, O Lord; and thy saints shall bless thee.

Psalms 145:8-10

M

THE FRIENDSHIP BOOK

AN old friend said to me the other day over a cup of coffee, "November is such a dreary, grey month — don't you agree, Francis?"

Well, on thinking about it, no, I didn't agree. I think that November is a month that has had a bad press.

I know November days are short, and can be dull, damp, and cold, but November can give us soft days of hazy, golden sunshine, blue skies, and glorious sunsets.

Crimson, scarlet, orange, and pink-berried shrubs brighten our gardens and parks, and the last roses of Summer overlap with the first flowers of Winter, for even Winter has its own flowers.

We can enjoy, too, the ever-changing tints of the countryside. Have you noticed the varying rich hues of brown in the freshly-ploughed fields?

Then in November clubs are getting into the swing of their Winter meetings and activities, and it is a month to enjoy the cosy, relaxing pleasures of our own fireside.

Isn't it easy to stick a label on someone or something without really stopping to consider if it is really deserved?

HAVE you noticed that old sayings mean different things to different people? For instance, there is the one: "Charity begins at home." It suggests to some that we should give to our own family first — starting and ending there.

I feel that the saying really means home is the place where charity should be taught and learned. What do *you* think?

THE FRIENDSHIP BOOK

THE busy scene at our bird table gives us endless entertainment, but one time I got quite exasperated. "What's the matter?" asked the Lady of the House.

"The sparrows chased away the blue tits and then a couple of blackbirds came along and chased off the sparrows. A bossy thrush has just frightened off a little hedge sparrow and now look at that crowd of starlings quarrelling amongst themselves. Why can't they all realise that there's plenty of food to go round?"

"Well, people aren't really any better, are they?" she said. "There are food surpluses in the West while poorer countries are starving. A lot of the hunger in the world is caused by unnecessary wars. If food supplies were fairly shared out between nations, there wouldn't be half the misery. So if *we* can't get it right, how do you expect the birds to?"

She hit the nail on the head, didn't she? I'm trying to be more understanding about the birds, while praying for greater peace across the globe.

WHY go to church? That's the question a preacher once asked. He answered it himself, this way.

A piece of coal comes alive in a fire. It becomes a burning ember in the midst of the blaze and plays its part in throwing out heat. Take it out of the fire, however, and it quickly cools and turns into a cinder, lifeless and dull.

Regular churchgoers, said the preacher, are like embers, glowing with warmth. Church members who don't go often — well, they are the cinders, cold and grey.

Embers and cinders . . . which are you?

FRIDAY—NOVEMBER 15.

INSTINCT

WHO tells a skein of geese to fly
Pattern-wise across the sky?
Those little ones of feathered breast,
Who tells them how to make their nest?
And batwing creatures, drab of hue,
Hang inverted all day through.
Who makes the owl to sleep by day
And fly by night to seek its prey?
If we would watch on Summer days
The insects have most wondrous ways
As indeed all creatures do,
So strange, we'd think it scarcely true.
I know what instinct is about,
The voice of God, without a doubt.

Barbara Jemison.

SATURDAY—NOVEMBER 16.

THE joy of the morning to you! Ahead of you is a magical twenty-four hours of new life to be filled, by YOU. It is yours, and yours alone. A precious possession. No one can take it from you — it is unstealable. What's more, no one receives more or less than *you* receive.

How's that for equality!

SUNDAY—NOVEMBER 17.

NOW thanks be unto God, which always causeth us to triumph in Christ, and maketh manifest the savour of his knowledge by us in every place.

Corinthians II 2:14

THE FRIENDSHIP BOOK

HERE are three quotations to think about today:

The greatest of faults is to think you have none.

Grudges are like babies — the more you nurse them, the bigger they will grow.

If Moses had been a committee, the children of Israel would still be in Sinai.

I LIKE the Church Army's paraphrase of St Paul's well-known sermon on love:

"Though I live in the most select neighbourhood and have all the latest mod-cons, without love I might as well dwell in a shack in the desert. I may have wall-to-wall carpets in every room, the most fashionable drapes and suites of French brocade, but without love these are as filthy rags.

"I may have a colour TV, a fully automatic kitchen and every electronic device, but without love, I am nothing.

"Love is children's fingerprints on the newly-painted walls, a doormat well used by welcome guests, a settee well seated. Love is sad when the doorbell is silent, when the telephone doesn't ring and when there is no-one with whom to share.

"Love does not come to an end when there is mud on the carpet; when a father spills paint in the sink; or when the dog scratches the front door.

"Bricks and mortar will one day be beyond repair; chrome and polish will quickly tarnish; gadgets find their way into the bin.

"BUT love . . . love goes on for ever."

THE FRIENDSHIP BOOK

THROUGHOUT the Summer and Autumn, young Michael had helped his mother to gather the fruits of the season. In July, they'd picked ripe, red raspberries; in September, dark and glistening brambles; and as October turned to November, they collected the last of the apples.

"What comes next?" Michael wanted to know.

"I think that's all for this year," said his mother. "At least, until it's time to pick a Christmas tree."

The little boy's eyes lit up. "What do we pick from Christmas trees?" he breathed. "Presents?"

IN one of his books, the English nature writer Richard Jefferies tried to define what he thought went into the making of a young girl:

"From all the enchanted things of earth and air, this preciousness has been drawn. From the south wind that breathed a century and a half over the green wheat; from the perfume of the growing grasses waving over heavy-laden clover and laughing veronica, hiding the greenfinches, baffling the bee; from the rose-lined hedge, woodbine and cornflower, azure blue, where yellowing wheat stalks crowd up under the shadow of green firs. All the devious brooklets' sweetness where the iris stays the sunlight; all the wild woods hold of beauty; all the broad hills of thyme and freedom . . . A hundred years of cowslips, bluebells, violets; purple Spring and golden Autumn; sunshine, shower, and dewy mornings . . ."

It's a long way from the old rhyme, "What are little girls made of?" Perhaps it's just as well that Jefferies didn't go on to say what goes into the making of young men!

THE FRIENDSHIP BOOK

ADVENTURERS STILL

WHAT happened to the two blithe hearts
  Who planned to roam the world?
Who schemed to buy a sailing ship
  With white sails all unfurled?
What happened to the two young tramps
Who roamed the high brown hills,
Who took the laughter and the tears
  And went all out for thrills?

What happened to that madcap pair?
  We're still the same two clowns,
We still can laugh, take in our stride
  All life's ups and downs.
Adventure now is life and love and
  Joy in each new day,
Slower now, but hand in hand, along life's
  Broad highway.

Georgina Hall.

WALKING through a shopping precinct, a bright yellow sticker caught my attention. It read: "Carpenter from Nazareth seeks joiners."

The most unusual job offer I have ever seen, but one with more rewards than most!

AND the dove came in to him in the evening; and, lo, in her mouth was an olive leaf pluckt off: so Noah knew that the waters were abated from off the earth.

Genesis 8:11

THE FRIENDSHIP BOOK

AMONG the hills of Derbyshire is a donkey sanctuary with a difference, for not only does it rescue sick and ill-treated donkeys, but also offers a respite to handicapped and under-privileged children. It is named the Michael Elliott Trust after the former actor and producer who founded it.

Donkeys are the gentlest and kindest of animals, ideal companions for children with special needs. When the Trust came into being, it was possible to accept visitors only on a daily basis, but now accommodation is available for children with a variety of handicaps, and they are able to have a week's holiday in the clean air near Buxton.

They respond very quickly to these docile animals and after a day of helping to feed, groom and care for them, the children spend the night just feet above where their own particular donkey is settling down.

To quote Annie Stirling, who runs the sanctuary with her husband John, "For these extraordinarily brave children, to spend seven days with an adopted donkey is the finest therapy on earth and I have seen it work in many different ways. It isn't until you've sat in a stable in the straw with a sick donkey, simply talking to and loving the animal, that the richness of the project becomes evident. The comfort of such an experience helps the child as much as it aids the donkey's recovery."

A truly worthwhile project.

THE secret of living? Theodore Roosevelt gave this simple recipe:

"Do what you can, with what you have, where you are."

SUNNY MEMORIES

THE FRIENDSHIP BOOK

AN elderly friend now in her eighties told me of a poem that her mother used to say when she felt tired — which she often did, as she had six children to care for and all the housework to do:

Here lies a poor woman who always was tired,
For she lived in a place where help wasn't hired.
Her last words on earth were, "Dear friends, I am going,
Where washing ain't done, nor sweeping, nor sewing,
And everything there is exact to my wishes,
For where they don't eat there's no washing of dishes . . .
Don't mourn for me now, don't mourn for me never,
For I'm going to do nothing for ever and ever!"

Fortunately, with all the labour-saving devices, young mothers should not be as overworked as they used to be, though I'm sure you will agree that bringing up a family and running a home is one of the most demanding jobs a woman can undertake — and one of the most satisfying, too.

A SMALL girl I know started Sunday school, and was asked by her teacher what she wanted to be when she grew up.

"An angel," replied Sarah firmly.

"That's very good," commended her teacher, much impressed. "And why do you want to be an angel?"

The small girl regarded her sternly. "So that I can fly round and drop water-bombs on people I don't like," she said.

I rather think that "little angel" has some way to go before she earns her wings!

OVER 100 years ago, a young man strolled into a Mexican village, and bewildered the natives simply because he looked so much like the statue of Jesus Christ, which stood in their chapel.

He was quite unaware of the interest in him, as he moved about the area looking for work . . . as a carpenter. This convinced the villagers even more that the young stranger was indeed a New Messiah, and they secretly gave thanks for this apparent "Second Coming".

Their attitudes started to change, slowly but surely, and although life in this particular area was far from idyllic, they seemed to play down the constant hazards they had to face — drought, disease, bandits, harvest failure. Selfishness and greed were gradually replaced by kindness and compassion, while hate and envy gave way to love and friendship.

Then one day, the young man was gone, leaving in his wake a group of inspired people, who had obviously been affected by his temporary presence. The strange thing was that he was an ordinary itinerant worker with no claims on being a "second Jesus", yet he had given them hope . . . that was the real miracle.

SATURDAY—NOVEMBER 30.

IN that splendid novel "War And Peace" written by Leo Tolstoy, I read — and re-read — this wise remark, and thought "how very true." Do you agree with Tolstoy — and me?

"Even in the best, most friendly and simple relations of life, praise and commendation are as indispensable as the oil which greases the wheels of a machine to keep them running smoothly."

DECEMBER

SUNDAY—DECEMBER 1.

A ND God gave Solomon wisdom and understanding exceeding much, and largeness of heart, even as the sand that is on the sea shore. And Solomon's wisdom excelled the wisdom of all the children of the east country, and all the wisdom of Egypt.

Kings I 4:29-30

MONDAY—DECEMBER 2.

M ISS SMITH hadn't been to church for years. "I've just got out of the habit," she would say. "Anyway, what's the point?"

Then she had a nasty fall and was confined to the house. Living alone, with no close friends, she feared things were going to be very difficult. However, to her surprise a woman she knew only by sight came to the door.

"I hear you've had an accident," she said. "Is there anything I can do? What about your shopping?"

Another woman brought her a lovely bunch of flowers, and a man two doors along offered to drive her to hospital for her check-ups.

They all rallied round and saw Miss Smith over her bad patch. What a relief it was for her, and what a surprise when she found that all three were members of a local congregation!

Now she knows what the point is. The point of going to church for these kind people was that they were willing to offer help when it was needed.

I hear that Miss Smith has joined their congregation. Who knows, one day she may find herself able to help someone else in need.

THE FRIENDSHIP BOOK

MY friend Ursula was born in Germany and has brought many traditions from her homeland to pass on to her children and grandchildren.

One of the special ones is the Advent wreath of evergreens set with red candles and placed on the tea-table on Advent Sunday, when the first of the candles is lit. Each following Sunday another candle is lit, then on Christmas Eve itself, the central candle blazes into light. It is a custom that has been observed from the 6th century.

In Ursula's home, the season of Advent is an important family time. All the children are invited for Sunday tea and as a candle is lit each week, the children are given a tiny gift — a few prettily-wrapped sweets, a coloured pencil or a lace handkerchief, perhaps. As Ursula said to me, "It's a simple ceremony that helps to explain to the little ones the true meaning of Christmas."

SISYPHUS was a mythical king of Corinth who was condemned forever to roll uphill a huge stone which rolled down again whenever it nearly reached the top. Never-ending effort — that was Sisyphus's life.

Even the ancients were familiar with frustrated endeavours. Like poor old Sisyphus, thousands of people down the ages have been thwarted, but have kept on trying.

So now, whenever things seem to go wrong and I feel like giving up, I picture this old Corinthian pushing away at his boulder — and I keep going as well.

There's nothing like perseverance and perhaps, unlike Sisyphus, our efforts will end — with success.

THE FRIENDSHIP BOOK

A GNES, although now in her eighties, is still able to recite poetry and takes an active interest in life beyond her front door. There is always a welcoming cup of tea at her cottage and she will usually have a little verse to hand to amuse me, or cause me to reflect a little.

I was still thinking about her latest verse as I travelled home one afternoon, and the next time I visited her, I took pen and paper and copied it down.

The more you give, the more you get,
The more you laugh, the less you fret,
The more you do unselfishly,
The more you live abundantly.
The more of everything you share,
The more you'll always have to spare,
The more you love, the more you'll find
That life is good and friends are kind.
For only what we give away
Enriches us from day to day.

How true these sentiments are!

T HE durian is a tropical fruit which grows in South-east Asia. It has a thick outer rind covered with sharp thorns, and such an unpleasant smell that it is banned on planes, trains and in many Asian hotels.

Yet, once the flesh has been reached it has a delicate, sweet flavour and can be eaten either raw or made into jam or ice-cream.

The durian is a fruit which the majority of us may not encounter, but it serves to remind us of the wisdom of not judging a book solely by its cover — or a person by outward appearance!

THE FRIENDSHIP BOOK

I PICKED up a magazine article recently about how to make the most of life.

Amongst the nuggets of advice was this one: "Be brave. Even if you're not, pretend to be. Nobody can tell the difference." Lady Sue Ryder, who along with her husband Leonard Cheshire, did so much for the Cheshire Homes, put it another way when she talked about "shutting out fear with all the strength of faith."

The actress Joan Plowright once wrote: "It's easy to deal with success and the good times. It's how you deal with the bad times that determines whether or not your life will be shaky." The epitaph she would have chosen for herself is "Buoyant In Adversity".

Whichever way we care to view it, the important thing is not what life brings to us, but what *we* bring to life. In the words of Sir Hugh Walpole:

" 'Tisn't life that matters!

'Tis the courage you bring to it."

AND walk in love, as Christ also hath loved us, and hath given himself for us an offering and a sacrifice to God for a sweetsmelling savour.

Ephesians 5:2

I WAS listening to a discussion on the radio about how we see ourselves when we reach a certain age. One speaker came up with an amusing and apt comment with conservation in mind:

"Let's not think of ourselves as being retired — but recycled!"

Now there's something to think about.

MAGNIFICENT

THE FRIENDSHIP BOOK

WALKING along a pathway one day, I spotted a glass bottle half buried in the verge. Ever mindful of the damage broken glass can do, I dug it out of the mud and undergrowth.

The bottle was whole, and to my surprise there was a plant inside. A measure of soil had been washed in, and in the soil had been a seed. A terrarium had been created by nature, the seed had sprouted and grown.

So it is in life — an unexpected cheery or comforting word, an unanticipated kindly deed, can take root and bear fruit in the life of a traveller along the world's highway.

MY CHILDHOOD

THERE were so many things of joy —
    The outings to the sea,
And all the treats ahead in store,
    The wonders yet to be!
The sledging on a snowy day
    Down steep, exciting hills,
And fireworks on the bonfire night —
    The thought of it still thrills!
The village shop at Christmastime,
    A fairy land delight,
The splendour of the Christmas tree,
    With bells and tinsel bright.
That solemn feeling when in church,
    The hymns that children sing,
So many precious joys to last —
    My childhood memories bring!

                    Elizabeth Gozney.

N

THE FRIENDSHIP BOOK

TWO men were walking past a church when they spotted a poster which proclaimed: "Blessed are the Meek."

"That's me to a T," said one of the men. "Yes, if there's one thing I pride myself on, it's my humility . . ."

I smiled to myself. How often we find that one of the hardest things we have to do is — see ourselves as others see us!

MRS HILDA ANDERSON of Thrapston, Northamptonshire, wrote this lovely poem for her Golden Wedding. Sadly, Mrs Anderson has since died, but Mr Anderson has given permission for me to publish it. It's called "All The Way".

God has brought us all the way
To this lovely Golden Day.
Our home would never be the same
Without the mention of His name,
So, we first thank the One above
For the blessing of His love,
Then, for the tender, loving care
Of the families who share
With us such precious days
In a million different ways.
For kindly friends and neighbours true,
For garden flowers of every hue,
For the seasons and the years
That brought us joy — and sometimes tears.
For the life we share together,
It unfolds in golden measure
The opportunity to say
God has brought us "all the way".

SATURDAY—DECEMBER 14.

OUR friend Ann was telling us of a delightful experience she witnessed in her church not long ago.

She was sitting beside a good friend who was accompanied by her six-year-old granddaughter. Lynn sat quietly between the two ladies and behaved beautifully during the service. Ann said that she had expected the little girl to fidget during the sermon, but she had continued to sit still.

After the final hymn, Ann heard Lynn whisper to her grandmother, "Grandma, I think that man really knows God."

Ann said that the preacher could not have been given a more fitting accolade for his preaching. Six-year-old Lynn had managed to express quite simply what the rest of the congregation felt.

SUNDAY—DECEMBER 15.

AND Mary said, Behold the handmaid of the Lord; be it unto me according to thy word. And the angel departed from her.

Luke 1:38

MONDAY—DECEMBER 16.

I RATHER like these optimistic lines by the American poet Longfellow:

For age is opportunity no less
Than youth itself, though in another dress,
And as the evening twilight fades away
The sky is filled with stars, invisible by day.

A rather beautiful way of saying, don't you think, that every age has its compensations and opportunities?

THE FRIENDSHIP BOOK

A NATURALIST spent time living in the most northerly region of Norway, studying the reindeer herds and the life of the Lapp people. He discovered that they had a centuries-old tradition which he thought explained why Father Christmas is said to visit homes by coming down chimneys.

During the darkness of the long Arctic night, while the majority of Lapps had sealed themselves into their tents to escape the bitter cold, travellers would cross the snow and ice bringing news, medicines and goods in their reindeer sleighs. The only way to enter or leave the tents once they had been sealed was by the smoke hole.

This, he thought, explained Santa's curious habit and it sounds convincing — but it still doesn't explain the sherry and the mince pies that are traditionally left for him!

HAVE you sent your Christmas cards yet? What a lovely custom it is, yet it seems to have started by accident.

In December 1843 a man called Henry Cole found he was late in writing the letters of Christmas greeting which he always sent to his friends. Since he did not have time to catch up with his Yuletide correspondence he asked an artist, Callcot Horsley, to design a card to send instead.

Other people saw the cards and, the following year, they wanted some, too. The custom spread quickly and in 1880 the Postmaster General had, for the first time, to make that now familiar plea, "Post early for Christmas!"

A PLACE
TO TREASURE

THE FRIENDSHIP BOOK

ONE Christmas season, General William Booth of the Salvation Army decided that he would send greetings to every Salvation Army unit scattered across the world. As the cost of cable messages was very expensive, he realised that he would have to restrict himself to just one word.

Which word would best express the spirit and challenge of the season?

After considerable thought, he made his choice and cabled his message. It was short and to the point. It read simply: "OTHERS".

CHRISTMAS SONG

SING a song of Christmas
A pocket full of love,
A song of trees and fairy lights
And one bright star above.
A song of joy and hopefulness
To lighten ev'ry heart,
To bring us all much closer,
Tho' we are miles apart.

Sing a song of Christmas
Of frankincense and gold,
And of the greatest story
That we were ever told.
It is the greatest message,
Enduring time and tears,
That we must love each other
Thro' the everlasting years.

Iris Hesselden.

THE FRIENDSHIP BOOK

ONE Winter's night Martin Luther was walking home along a lonely road when, looking up, he saw a bright star poised above a fir tree. It reminded him of the Star of Bethlehem, and when he got home he cut off the top of a tree, brought it into the house and fixed a candle to its topmost point.

Nowadays most of us have a Christmas tree in the house, and beautiful many of them are, but I never think they look complete without a star on top to remind us of the wonderful journey and the amazing sight at the end of it — the Babe in the manger.

Martin Luther's moment of inspiration has brought joy into countless homes and hearts.

NOW when Jesus was born in Bethlehem of Judaea in the days of Herod the king, behold, there came wise men from the east to Jerusalem, Saying, Where is he that is born King of the Jews? for we have seen his star in the east, and are come to worship him.

Matthew 2:1-2

HERE is a thought for today:
"There are many happinesses, both great and small, which brighten our lives, but surely friendly words and ways add sunniness to all our days."

And here's another thought for tomorrow:

Make new friends
But keep the old.
The new are silver
The old are gold.

THE FRIENDSHIP BOOK

YOU may have heard before of the Nativity play in which a small boy had set his heart on being one of the Wise Men, but was deeply disappointed and annoyed to be given the part of the innkeeper instead.

That's why he introduced an unscripted amendment to the official version, and when Joseph knocked at his door, he replied, "Come in, there's plenty of room!"

Joseph was equal to the occasion, however. He poked his head inside, had a quick look round, and retorted, "I'm not taking my wife into a place like that. Come on, Mary, we'll sleep in the stable."

DOLLY lived in Manchester with her father Dr John Byrom, a Fellow of Trinity College Cambridge, who had gone back to live in his native city.

Dolly always sent greetings cards to her friends at Christmas, and would ask her father to write a verse for them. In 1750 he wrote a complete hymn.

One of Dolly's friends liked it so much that she passed it on to Mr Wainwright, the Cathedral organist. He borrowed it, and quickly composed the tune called "Yorkshire" which is still sung to Dr Byrom's "Christians Awake".

That same cold Christmas Eve the Manchester Cathedral choir walked to the Byrom residence, and on the stroke of midnight for the very first time in the open air "Christians Awake, Salute The Happy Morn" was sung. The author was soon awake and was greatly surprised when he heard his own words!

These words still make Christmas morning magical for us today as we arise to adore Him.

THURSDAY—DECEMBER 26.

THE way we view the first snowfall of the Winter depends to a large extent on our age group. Youngsters are filled with excitement — the anticipation of lots of fun with snowball fights and sledge rides — while older people may think only about the cold and inconvenience.

I try to see it through the eyes of Ogden Nash who described the magic thus:

Winter is the king of showmen,
Turning tree stumps into snowmen
And houses into birthday cakes
And spreading sugar over lakes.

Will you join me as I view the scene? It can make such a difference.

FRIDAY—DECEMBER 27.

TROUBLE rhymes with bubble — and vanishes just as quickly!

Anon.

SATURDAY—DECEMBER 28.

ONE of my lifelong friends once said to me, "It helps to look on the bright side and have a sense of humour as you get older, don't you think, Francis?"

I did, but I would say a sense of humour, with the ability to laugh at ourselves and the ways of the world, is priceless at *any* stage of our life. A touch of humour, a little laughter, and a generous dash of optimism, can diffuse many of life's trying moments, and bring a sense of proportion to many things.

THE FRIENDSHIP BOOK

IN the beginning God created the heaven and the earth. And the earth was without form, and void; and darkness was upon the face of the deep. And the Spirit of God moved upon the face of the waters.

Genesis 1:1-2

GETTING OLDER

"IT'S awful getting older,"
I often hear folk say
As they recount their aches and pains,
Which will not go away.

But it's helpful to remember,
When considered overall
That if we didn't reach old age,
We'd not be here at all!

Dorothy M. Loughran.

IN the last days of December a few clumps of early snowdrops flower without fail in the coldest and most windswept part of my garden.

Elegant and taller than their later sisters, the snowdrops bloom for a number of weeks, shrugging off snow and icy rain, and sharp white frost.

They are a beautiful bridge between the Twelve Days of Christmas and the first hint of Spring, their flowering a lovely beginning to a new year, and yet a small happening in a big world.

However, often it is these little things in life which give much pleasure and happiness, don't you think?

Where The Photographs Were Taken

WHITE AND BRIGHT — *Troutbeck, Cumbria.*
LAKE LAND — *The River Wey, Guildford.*
MIST OPPORTUNITIES — *Windermere from Lough Rigg.*
MOUNTAIN MAJESTY — *Shieldaig, Wester Ross.*
SPRING SERENADE — *Deene Hall, Northamptonshire.*
LONDON LIGHTS — *Westminster.*
GUARDIAN OF THE SEAS — *South Stack, Holy Island, Anglesey.*
HORSES TO WATER . . . — *Lorna Doone Farm, Devon.*
IN PASTURES GREEN — *Pitcombe, Somerset.*
PATHWAY TO PEACE — *Dove Dale, Derbyshire.*
GLEN OF DREAMS — *Glen Etive, Argyll.*
QUIET WATERS — *Bridge of Sighs, Cambridge.*
SUMMER DREAM — *Lizard Point, Cornwall.*
A WAY OF LIFE — *Bray, Berkshire.*
ROSES ARE RED, SKIES ARE BLUE . . . — *Scarborough.*
AT REST — *River Avon at Stratford.*
BRIDGE OF SMILES — *Tower Bridge, London.*
GONE FISHING — *Llyn Crafnant, Gwynedd.*
SAND, SEA AND SUMMER — *Bedruthan Steps, Cornwall.*
PARADISE VALLEY — *Selworthy, Somerset.*
LEAVES AND EAVES — *Swan Green, Hampshire.*
MY FEATHERED FRIENDS — *River Wye, Bakewell.*
CAMARADERIE — *The Oxford Canal, Napton.*
MAGNIFICENT — *York.*
A PLACE TO TREASURE — *Derwentwater.*
DIVINE DECEMBER — *Ardington, Oxfordshire.*

ACKNOWLEDGEMENTS: **Ivan Belcher;** Pathway To Peace, Quiet Waters, At Rest, My Feathered Friends, Camaraderie, Divine December. **Paul Felix;** Spring Serenade, In Pastures Green. **V. K. Guy;** On The Right Road, White And Bright, Mountain Majesty, London Lights, Guardian Of The Seas, Horses To Water . . ., Glen Of Dreams, Summer Dream, Roses Are Red, Skies Are Blue . . ., Bridge Of Smiles, Sand Sea And Summer, Magnificent, A Place To Treasure, Mist Opportunities. **Picturepoint;** Daddy's Girl. **Kenneth Scowen;** You'll Find Me In The Garden, Paradise Valley, Sunny Memories. **Derek G. Widdicombe;** Gone Fishing. **Andy Williams;** Lake Land, A Way Of Life, Leaves And Eaves.

Printed and Published by D. C. THOMSON & CO., LTD.,
185 Fleet Street, London EC4A 2HS.
© D. C. THOMSON & Co., Ltd., 1995

ISBN 0-85116-608-3